KNIGHTS AND KNAVES OF AUTUMN

40 YEARS OF PRO FOOTBALL AND THE MINNESOTA VIKINGS

by Jim Klobuchar

Dedication

This is for SCW, who loves books and reminded the author that her innocence in pro football does not deter her from reading about pro football, for which thank heavens.

Book design by Jonathan Norberg

Published by Adventure Publications
P.O. Box 269
Cambridge, MN 55008
1-800-678-7006

ISBN 1-885061-84-6

Acknowledgements

With Thanks

The author and publisher wish to express their appreciation to a number of people and organizations who provided their assistance and good will in the publication of this book. We especially would like to thank Steve Anderson of the Ross and Haines company for its courtesy in allowing the use of some material that originally appeared in *True Hearts and Purple Heads*, by Jim Klobuchar, published initially by Ross and Haines. Our thanks also go to Jeff Siemon, the former Viking star who collaborated with Jim in the publication of *Will the Vikings Ever Win the Super Bowl?* a small portion of which appears in this book, and Fran Tarkenton, who collaborated with Jim in the publication of *Tarkenton*, excerpts of which appear in this book. We also thank Wheelock Whitney and Mike Lynn, both former executives of the Vikings, for making time available to reflect on issues during their stewardships; Jerry Burns, the former Viking coach for his pungent comments on episodes in his pro football career; Bob Hagen and the Viking organization for their generosity in making photos available; and Barbara Schmitt for her flawless technical advice in the reproduction of the text via disks and computers and all the mysteries of cyberspace, a field in which the author pleads almost total ignorance.

Preface

Late in the Vikings' playoff loss in St. Louis last winter, Randy Moss grabbed a bottle of drinking water on the Viking sideline and squirted an official.

Never mind that the defeat was the team's latest nosedive in its long and dark-starred pursuit of the Super Bowl. Moss' brainless assault on the official gave the Viking performance some redeeming value in the theater. It came straight out of the romper room, although preschoolers have behaved more maturely. The National Football League keeps no squirt bottle statistics to verify that this was a record distance for spraying an official. Record or not, it was a typical brat behavior by a hugely gifted young football player who threatens never to grow up. A subsequent $50,000 fine imposed by the league could hasten that process, although considering Moss' brief history in the NFL, it's not likely.

Randy Moss, I decided at that moment, was a kind of welcome missing link for me. He was a connection, a bridge between the then-and-now of football, between the scruffy vagabonds of 40 years ago and the millionaire nomads of today. Randy was a windfall, somebody who genuinely deserved superstar status but was still capable of impulsively goofy acts to match the screwball acts of the football mediocrities that I'd found so endearing over the years. The players I remembered from my earlier years of football writing were rich in offbeat behavior. Most of the eccentric ones in today's football are wealthy hams who strut for the cameras before the play is finished or do pelvic vibrations to celebrate a simple tackle. Most of these graceless gyrations make me retch. But Moss is a different kind of eccentric. Here is one who is actually worth the millions but has to fight to stay awake during the game because he is a self-absorbed, precocious kid who bores easily and runs recklessly toward his own goal line after catching a punt. He does this to be creative, gambling to break a long run. He also does it because running straight ahead to gain yards looks tedious. On this count alone, Moss would have belonged with the oddballs I remembered from 40 years ago. You don't have to like oddballs to be able to identify them. Palmer Pyle, though, was a guy who was easy to love.

Pyle once built a fire behind the Viking bench to avert frostbite in a game in New York. I don't know if Moss could match Pyle in conflagrations, but he does lead in adolescent behavior and casual arrogance.

Like you, I watch most of my football today from the couch. For me it sets off inner wars between my admiration for the skills of today's playing millionaires and my distaste for some of the grotesque posturing they do, the mugging and the grandstanding. I'm gratified that the industry is now paying its players money that makes them independent. But I'm appalled by the abuse of those riches by some of the players who take the money and coast or stonewall their teams for more. I'm also appalled by the football industry's routine exploitation of the TV audience's hunger to watch the game, an exploitation that takes the form of extortion–forcing taxpayers to build lavish football arenas so the ownership barons can make more millions.

In the 40 years since I first wrote pro football, the game has gained enormous visibility. Most of that is deserved. The game packs a powerful wallop in the clash of great athletes, in the mix of its strategies and skills and personalities, and its fundamental law-of-the-jungle fight for competitive survival.

This book will lift you back into some of the Katzenjammer days of the pro football I remember fondly, and spans the eras into the new millennium so that a Cris Carter would not be misplaced as a hero in the 1960s as well as the 1990s. The difference is that Cris Carter makes a fortune today where he would have made $15,000 then, and as one of the wealthier evangelists in town, he is moved to salute God Almighty after each touchdown. It's very doubtful that Norm Van Brocklin would have completely understood this ritual 40 years ago.

The pro football of my early years in the newspaper business was the football of characters who seemed to be drawn as much from vaudeville and James Thurber as they were from the huddle. You will meet some of them in this book, as you will Carter and Moss and Jeff George and a few dozen others for whom today's football has become a money tree to surpass all of the fables of inexhaustible wealth that we learned in school.

In September of 1961, the Minnesota Vikings played the Chicago Bears at Metropolitan Stadium in Bloomington, Minnesota, in a game that was modestly described as historic. It brought major league professional football to Minnesota. But on that weekend there were no massive parades from the downtowns of Minneapolis and St. Paul to the squat little arena on the edge of the prairie. Nobody even considered a parade from downtown Bloomington, because there *was* no downtown Bloomington.

From the higher galleries and the press box that day you could scan acres of cornfields to the south, stalks waving in the breeze. If you got out your binoculars you could see John Deere tractors running around. It was a lovely pastoral scene but there were no caravans of TV teams to pan the landscape or to deliver a Bob Costas-style poetic narrative to record the immortality of the event. Nobody used rhetoric like that in the television of the 1960s. Some of the announcers, in fact, couldn't tell a blitz from a blintz and you didn't have three men in the booth and Lesley Visser on the sidelines to take your mind off the commercials. Plus the empty seats at the kickoff of that Vikings-Bears game tended to tone down any symptoms of an immortal event.

In the 1960s pro football was beginning to captivate the American public. But no one could foresee that it would become the overwhelming multi-billion dollar powerhouse of American athletics that it is today. Pro football still had a rustic tinge then, a game not so far removed from leather helmets, nickel-and-dime wages and the haystacks of its incubator years.

Yet there was an undeniably historic quality in the Vikings-Bears game of 40 years ago. It was the first game for the Minnesota Vikings, who in this improbable hour beat the Chicago Bears, the onetime Midway Monsters and the most celebrated franchise in pro football. But I remember the faces more than the result. I remember George Halas prowling the Chicago Bears' sidelines, swearing and bellowing at the officials almost as venomously as he ripped his stumbling football team. I remember the Viking coach, Norm Van Brocklin, doing the same thing a few yards away on the same sideline. The layout of the quirky little Met didn't allow enough room for player benches on opposite sidelines. Because his team was winning, Van Brocklin was less venomous than Halas, but not much. He did manage to call one official a pervert (not audible to the official) and another official a "spaghetti-eater," which is what Van Brocklin called all Italians, although it wasn't quite clear whether in the heat of battle Van Brocklin knew the difference between Italians and Greeks. It was also clear that it didn't matter to the Dutchman. He was capable of slandering each with equal malice.

I also remember the faces of the aging halfback, Hugh McElhenny, still running with that incomparable grace, and Fran Tarkenton, playing with dash and a streak of gall, throwing four touchdown passes in his first game as a pro.

I remembered something else. All four of them later entered the football's Hall of Fame.

So yes, it was a landmark day for football and I suppose for me. My reminiscences of it with a newspaper crony nudged me to write this book. Part of it is drawn from some of the daffiest adventures of early Minnesota Viking football, set down in a book I wrote in 1970, *True Hearts and Purple Heads*.

It was described by the publishers, Ross and Haines, as the unauthorized biography of a football team, but most of it could just as well have been pulled from the scenarios of Bugs Bunny.

They were the days when a team's star fullback and defensive end would routinely sign on with the highway department with picks and shovels when the season was over. They made eight grand for playing football and had to pour asphalt to keep groceries on the table. Today the star fullback and defensive end start the off-season checking *The Wall Street Journal* and their financial advisers about how to handle their $4 million signing bonus.

So the question then becomes: Where is pro football today when it is the Goliath of American athletics? Is it a better game for all of the money and its heightened popularity? Are the players better, the game more entertaining, the owners wiser, greedier or both?

While it is sentimentally connected to those faces and the random looniness of the earlier times, this book explores some of those new-millennium questions and tries to scatter some fun and spasms of insight here and there. It also scans the Vikings' latest miseries in the 1999 playoffs and tries to foresee what may be ahead for this team corporately. I wrote football off and on for nearly 20 years. Most of that was hard-core, sports page writing for the football zealots, and I enjoyed that hugely. In my other years as a general columnist for the Minneapolis newspaper, I took a kind of smuggler's satisfaction in bringing the game before people who were more conditioned to reading politics or bedroom squabbles. And for a substantial part of that time I also smuggled some of my uneven wisdom into the lives of thousands of women in a football clinic that was wild and hilarious and raucous and, I'll have to say, even valuable to the inquisitive scholars now and then.

Football brought into my life in newspapering a special flavor and rolling bafflement over the human condition as it was expressed in the faces and struggles of those helmeted brawlers. It was always a surprise to learn that away from the battle, most of them were very much like you and me in their yearnings, their anxieties, their follies and their fears. Reading this book is not likely to damage your ongoing education in the game if you're one of the experts, and it might twitch your interest in an earlier era if you're too young to remember the Van Brocklins and Palmer Pyles. If you are, you might take a moment to grieve their disappearance from the glitzy football we see today, for all of its quality and its wealth.

Jim Klobuchar, August 2000

"A few guys hated him. . . . But they would have died rather than not play for him. They needed his approval. His personality was that powerful."

—*Paul Hornung commenting on Vince Lombardi.*

Billion Dollar Football— What Have We Lost?

*T*he Golden Boy, Paul Hornung, abdicated years ago as the resident Adonis of pro football. He did that with heartfelt reluctance. If you were once the prince of the night parlors around the National Football League, you don't give up that exalted status without regret.

But here he was, back on camera in a TV studio in the fall of 1999 with white locks flowing and an impressive gut, recycled as a sage and ancient mariner of pro football.

The issue of the hour was the impact of megabucks on the pro football game Hornung once revered. Never mind his reputation as one of its ranking after-hours rascals when he played. Hornung's code on the field was hard and uncompromising. He played each down faithful to the code. The men he respected on both sides of the line played the same way. Later, at the reunions, they laughed at some of the slogans: "Guts and All." "Going to the Wall." But they played the game by those hairy axioms. The question: Did today's boys of autumn, watching the stock markets as avidly as the Monday morning stats, pound the line as ferociously and party together as exuberantly as the musketeers of pro football's greening years in Hornung's time? Did they feel the same loyalty?

So here was a pro football Hall of Famer, Hornung, a Heisman Trophy winner, broadcaster and retired boulevardier, now in his mid-60s. He was conscripted by the cable channel to tell us where the colossus of pro football was going into the new millennium and how it got to be uncontrollable.

He passed the first and only true test of the designated sage.

He didn't know how pro football got to be uncontrollable.

But he knows it is. And because of that he grieved about it, he said, along with a few thousand other old pros. Although he was a marvelous and hard-willed football player, outside the arena Hornung could be a scamp and a man of some impressive past sins. Hypocrisy never seemed to be one of them. I always liked him for that. And now he mourned pro football's fixation with big money, but he spared the viewer any needless piety. He said he really didn't know if he would act any differently than the billionaires who own the game today, or the millionaires who play it. What he meant was that if the money was there and if it meant dumping the team he played for, he'd probably go after the bigger dough.

He could be loyal to the Packers and Fuzzy Thurston and Vince Lombardi in the 1960s, he seemed to be saying. But could he profess the same love for the old Titletown, U.S.A., the frozen streets of Green Bay, and Speed's Bar if he was a free agent in the year 2000? And Jerry Jones in Dallas was on the horn and saying, "Hot damn, Paulie, how about $25 mill for four years and a $12 mill signing bonus?"

Yet what seemed to be bothering him more about football today wasn't its creation of a whole new breed of gypsy millionaires, but what that phenomenon meant to the emotional side of the game he remembered. The game he remembered were his days in Green Bay, Lombardi's scowl, lining up with Jim Taylor, roughhousing in the locker room with Hawg Hanner, Jerry Kramer and Willie Davis.

On this particular day, Hornung was the fifth or sixth of the old pro lions who came through the revolving door of the sports channels. Today's sports television can't get enough of the embattled old faces and the marquee names. They dress up a half hour show and give it credibility.

In television's obsession with pro football today, this is a benign and handy fate that eventually overtakes most old pros who are glib or whose fame has a long shelf life. We should applaud. Everyone wants to feel needed but not everybody gets reincarnated on national television after being washed out of the business years ago. A lot of these people are my old pals. They are the used-up heroes of the football industry, some of them still relatively famous and prosperous, some of them gimping along on the pension plan's margins.

Forty years ago they might have been pumping gas as a career change. Today they are pursued by TV producers who want to make the next 30 minutes sound fresh and opinionated and, with luck, a little outrageous. TV prowls the phone books and casting offices for them. Sometimes it tries the nursing homes. Television's saturation of America with pro football today is ruthless. The game seems compelling to enough Americans to push TV into 24-hour a day coverage. No relief is granted. If you turn on the set, television takes no prisoners and grants no escape. From September to February it is wall-to-wall football. If you turn off the television set it's there on Internet and a thousand web sites. If you click off the Internet it's in the morning paper—profiles, posters and a crazy, virtual reality football game created from cyberspace. If that's not enough, you get one more quote from a belligerent cornerback who knows how to stop the generally unstoppable Randy Moss.

All of this is a million dollars' worth of free advertising for pro football in the newspaper, for the Minnesota Vikings, let's say. It's also free advertising for television, and for the peddlers who push team merchandise. But the newspaper doesn't look at it that way. The appeal of pro football is so broad and deep, it will say, the hysteria so widespread that the public's appetite *cannot* be fully fed. And unless the newspaper is out in front of the hysteria, it will be dumped into the ditch of irrelevance by its media competitors. And those include and sometimes are led by the ultimate hysterics, the talk shows.

There were other faces and voices on that show where Paul Hornung was a guest. But Hornung's face and voice were the ones that drew me. It wasn't so much that we were acquainted, first when he played for the Packers and I wrote pro football for the Minneapolis newspaper. Later we had endless gab sessions in the hotel coffee shops and bars in his years as a broadcast analyst covering the Vikings. No, what attracted me to Hornung's testimony on that show was the utter futility of this aging warhorse and after-hours rake, trying to get some grip on the winds of change in a pro ball culture he once knew so well. But look at it now! What was it? A runaway monster in the entertainment business, sucking up and spitting out millions of dollars daily and engulfing the television screens, almost comic in its hypnotic hold on the sporting public. Societies of nuns went to pro football games. So did caravans of tourists from Japan, and they could probably tell you Cris Carter's average yards per catch. And why was Paul Hornung feeling futile?

He didn't know how pro football was ever going to regain its fundamental character of another time. Somebody on the show actually called it "soul."

Maybe we ought to stop right there.

Are we serious about pro football with a soul? We're talking about a game played today by 300-pound tycoons wearing gold earrings, by acrobatic prodigies who can mug a defensive back at the height of their leap, grab the ball with one hand and come down with both feet in bounds. It is a game whose players in 1999 included one accused of trying to murder the mother of his unborn child. A second player, one of the game's best linebackers, was accused of murder a few weeks later. Another, drafted on the first round by the Vikings, tried to cut his throat in the despair of emotional problems. It's a game in which the hooliganism on the field in 1999 (loony celebrations, helmet-to-helmet mayhem) matches some of the arrests for solicitation and drug use off the field.

Can this kind of game harbor a soul under the sweat and blood and casual vulgarity and mounting concussions? To this add immature college dropouts who become millionaires before playing a down in the NFL.

For some players, it can and does have a soul.

Hornung didn't use the word. But it's probably what he meant when he said "camaraderie," which is a safer word for an ex-stud to use when he's talking about feelings on TV. Thank God he avoided "chemistry." But Hornung knew that today's ballplayers, for all of their wealth, are capable of experiencing camaraderie, when they are in the midst of a two-minute drive to the goal line in a big game, or sharing the exhilaration of an approaching Super Bowl. He was talking about remembered years when that feeling seemed to go deeper. It was the bond of grown men playing a kid's game in dead earnest year after year, understanding the others' quirks and goofball flights, appreciating the others' refusal to yield to pain.

And when their careers were finished, they would remember those years and the respect that grew among them and never waned with time. Hornung sounded wistful. Today's game was still good and exciting. Obviously. The ratings were huge. The public couldn't get enough. The athletes were as good or better than ever. If you played pro football today, and you were good at it, maybe only good enough to perform one special act well, you could get rich. You could get there if you did no more than center the ball accurately for punts and field goals.

And yet–

The old system might have been lousy and tyrannical in forcing ball players to work for the same owners until they got too old or slow to make the team. But the old system did make them a team. And maybe in the long run, that was better than the big money.

The camera was kind to Paul Hornung. From the privacy of the lounge in my den I applauded that, too. He was now in his ripe years and the butter-colored hair of his hell-raising days had bleached with his approaching dotage. But it was still impeccably swept back in a meringue of white waves. No doubt about it, this guy was still a star and the camera seemed to acknowledge it with some accent lighting on the Golden Boy's profile—and the puzzlement in his eyes. He'd been impaneled as one of the elders of pro football to give the ballplayers' evaluation of the state of the industry at the turn of the millennium. He shared the dais with another one of pro football's midcentury heavyweights, the Los Angeles Rams' Deacon Jones, a defensive lineman who terrorized quarterbacks for a decade. They were joined by two of the game's modern Midases, Tim Brown of the Oakland Raiders and Mike Strahan of the New York Giants, both of them current, active and counting.

It was good and thoughtful television, especially by today's standards of round-the-clock, often sappy and always relentless midweek pro football hype. Deacon and the Golden Boy tried hard not to come across as old crocks crusading for the restoration of a time now vanished. Yeah, money has turned the game's stars into pricey jocks-for-rent. What are you going to do? Tell them not to take the money? You weren't going to tell that to Tim Brown or Mike Strahan, two of the top-echelon stars of today's NFL and both of them capable of playing with Hornung and Deacon on anybody's team, in anybody's era. But Brown looked pensive. Rich, but pensive. He thought that was an appealing idea, playing for one team, start to finish, from rookie season to retirement. It would be nice, he suggested, if Al Davis, the Raiders' owner, would let him finish his career in Oakland.

Meaning, if Al stacked up enough money to give Timmy a decent chance to turn down all of the millions, he would attract in free agency.

Hornung seemed to blink. He admired Tim Brown, a Golden Domer from another generation, a Heisman winner at Notre Dame nearly 30 years after Hornung did it himself. But it all looked surreal. What were they talking about here? Ballplayers make $5 and $6 million a year, but it wasn't enough. It wasn't enough because somebody was going to offer more. And sure, it was good football. Steve Young, Terrell Davis, Deion Sanders, Emmitt Smith, Troy Aikman, Warren Sapp, all those guys making the big money could play in any era, and play hard and win.

But Hornung, the pragmatist, couldn't say what he wanted to say. He conceded that the game might be faster, the athletes today bigger and stronger, the techniques better. The offenses were more sophisticated and the defenses smarter. And pro ball had never been more popular. But somehow it was better 40 years ago.

Not that the game was necessarily better. So what was better? Maybe the times, the old circle-the-wagons mentality of guys who had played together for years and who knew how to cover for a lineman who was playing on one good leg, not only knew how to cover for him but did it on every play.

I got up and went into some old files in the garage. There was a copy there of a piece I wrote for the NFL's *Game Day* magazine in 1986. It was one of those stories that John Wiebusch of *Game Day* wanted in the magazine every three or four years, about the growing legend of (who else?) Vince Lombardi. I called Hornung in Louisville. As we talked, we each inevitably drew a mental picture of the coach Hornung always called The Old Man: Lombardi with the archetypal southern Italian face, a broad pug nose and dark, inquisitive eyes that harbored something smoldering, almost glowing, inside them. I told Hornung that if Hollywood had cast *The Godfather* in the 1960s, Lombardi would have beaten out Marlon Brando for the title role. Hornung laughed raucously. I said if they would have given Lombardi two months with the script, he would have outacted Brando. He laughed harder. It wasn't because the line was funny. He laughed because he thought it was true.

Every few years, sometime around the Super Bowl, when the audiences are the biggest, the networks rewind the Vince Lombardi saga, and somehow it always seems worth it each time. Why? In a business filled with transitory heroes, Lombardi remains the idealization both of a game and a creed, this man of such consuming, irreversible commitment.

"Tell me about Lombardi and those years of pro ball," I said to Hornung.

"He really talked the way you see it on those plaques," Paul Hornung said. "'Winning isn't everything, it's the only thing.'" I don't care if he didn't invent that slogan. The slogan was more Lombardi than it was whoever said it first. He said those things in our squad meetings and in the locker room. But he didn't do it with just words. There was nothing magic about his language. It was the way he dominated every room he walked into and everything he did. He was obsessed with doing it right, which means winning. A lot of coaches are. This guy knew how to win. He did it every place and in every weather. He got into your skin. For most of the guys who played for him he somehow became the most important person in the world. He screamed and he threatened you and intimidated you. A few guys hated him for that. But they would have died rather than not play for him. They needed his approval. His personality was that powerful.

"You know, some guys, after they die, get bigger. The stories about them, especially if they were super successful people, inflate their personalities and what they did. It's not that way with Lombardi. He was big *then*. For 10 years he was pro football in America, and he deserved that image. He walked into a small city in Wisconsin and took a bunch of guys going nowhere and turned them into one of the greatest football teams ever put together. It's not only that he did it, but the way he did it. He had values and ethics that went right to the core of what it takes and what it means to be a successful human being as well as a successful athlete. Yeah, he ranted and insulted. But when he talked about love on a football team–before everybody else did it and it got to be a cliché–he found a way to make that understood and believable. He wasn't talking about hugging. That was not exactly a huge thing in his life. He was talking about the sacrifices you had to make for each other, and about what the other player was going through when he was in pain or in some struggle.

"Everybody who played for him was forever changed by him in some way, and changed for the good, even if they didn't care for him. How many people can you say that about?"

For most of us, it's a short list. Maybe some of the saints are on it. But Lombardi certainly wasn't one of those. Ego? Yes, of course. Hornung cherishes his private encounters with Lombardi both when he played and in later years when Lombardi had moved on to Washington, D.C.

"I remember walking into a Washington restaurant with him. He got a standing ovation from the diners. It was a big and fancy restaurant and they all stood up. And when we got to our table, he couldn't resist. He had ego enough to appreciate all that. He said, 'Paul, how do you like it? This town is full of some of the biggest politicians in the world, and nobody notices. But the football coach walks in, and everybody applauds.'"

But they don't applaud every football coach. Lombardi knew that. He didn't have to say it. So what Hornung seemed to be lamenting on that TV show, far more than the game's takeover by the money god, was the erosion of the game's brotherhood. When free agency came and the salaries started soaring, the football hierarchs had to put in some kind of meaningful salary cap to survive their own spasms of covetousness–wanting to win so badly they could bankrupt the team in bidding wars. The best teams now couldn't hold onto all of their stars nor even to some of the role players. They had to limit the number of tycoons they could afford. And often the fallout of that arrangement was a ruinous rivalry among some of the star position players on the team. If your status depended on the number of passes you caught, so did your earning power. And if you didn't catch enough passes to maintain your status, you were going to grumble. The quarterback was the fall guy, or the offensive coordinator, or the other guys who caught passes. It happens all the time in a pro football society of today where cash is king. And there goes the brotherhood.

And why was he smiling, this old crock of the newspaper city room, while Paul Hornung was lamenting? I was smiling because Hornung and I were on the same page. The pro football Hornung knew was the pro football I knew. I didn't know the inside game the way Hornung knew it, but I knew the players and the times. I knew the wackiness of it and the random brutality of it, the mediocre grunts who were usually the stars of the locker-room brawls because the stars were smart enough to get out of there before the blood flowed. But was there a special kind of brotherhood then? Yes, although it wasn't especially noticeable if the team went 0-for September and October. And were there characters then? True characters and not necessarily the loudmouth characters of the Shannon Sharpe shticks?

Lord, there were characters. So maybe for a while we can shut down all the dot coms on the Internet, and shut off Jaws Jaworski. (On what cable is Jaws tonight? How can you remember them all?) And we can revert ourselves to the early 1960s, when pro football was still a game and not a billion dollar sideshow and soap opera. And if the team you were watching was the first Minnesota Vikings, it was something a little more than a game. It was close to an end-to-end trauma, which not only deserved the fans' sympathy but their bewilderment.

Let's look in on this dysfunctional family and its slightly maniacal first coach.

"I'm clearing out. I choose life."

—Viking rookie in a farewell note to his roommate, explaining why he was forfeiting a $1,000 signing bonus to escape from Norm Van Brocklin's scorched earth training camp regimen.

The Dutchman's Reign of Terror

*I*n their formative years, the Minnesota Vikings practiced in a training camp in the northern Minnesota jack pines. If you watched them day to day, or night to night, there was always a serious question about their identity. Was this a football team or a wildlife refuge?

Most of the inmates of Norm Van Brocklin's first training camps at Bemidji were socially rowdy and professionally unloved. Almost all of them were dismissed as aimless mediocrities by the evaluators of pro football flesh. Others were actual basket cases, quietly hostile and antisocial, brooding over their fate in landing on a football team coached by Van Brocklin. The Dutchman was that rare combination of a football genius and a reconstituted Attila. His reputation hung like a malevolent cloud over these football orphans who'd been abandoned by their former keepers in the NFL and left to wonder whether they would ever again experience a normal life after the Devil's Island of Van Brocklin's training camp.

On the other hand, there were actually some living, breathing, identifiable football players in Van Brocklin's custody. Not all of them schemed escape. Many of them became authentic stars. Francis Tarkenton began his 18 Hall of Fame years on the first day of the Vikings' first camp in July of 1961, tossing a football to Bob Schnelker, one of the 36 players made available to the Vikings in the expansion draft of 1961. This was the group of derelicts more or less immortalized by Van Brocklin as "the 36 stiffs." That was Van Brocklin's idiom. He was on most days abusive and profane, cruel and paranoid. Yet at times when he saw a player struggling and trying hard to make it but doomed to the waiver wire by some inadequacy he couldn't overcome, Van Brocklin seemed almost compassionate. He knew the pro football offense as almost no one else. He won as a quarterback in the

National Football League partly by bullying and terrorizing his own team-mates. He did it by carving up the man-to-man defenses of that era with his arm, his brains and his unflinching will. He did it in the belief that Norm Van Brocklin could beat any football team and any quarterback with the guts to think differently. But the lodge of pro football—the fellowship of those who belonged—nourished his fondness for the game as it did Paul Hornung, and it sometimes tickled him. He giggled and roared over the stories when he relaxed. And some days early in the Vikings' beginnings he would walk into a players' bull session on the second floor of Pine Hall at Bemidji. He figured out a way to get a couple of six-packs into the room (never a very intricate problem) and he candidly fraternized with players he had dressed down unmercifully in the scrimmage a few hours before. At that hour they were all lodge brothers, and the coach and his players were equals.

So when Tarkenton showed up on the first day, to begin a relationship between the two that ultimately became destructive and filled with poison, Van Brocklin playfully cuffed him on the head and called him Georgia Peach and P.K. for Preacher's Kid. In a few days he was calling him one of the smartest rookie quarterbacks he had ever seen. Five years later he was calling him a son of a bitch.

The Viking rosters even in their earliest years were dappled with players of distinction, then or later in their careers—Tarkenton, Hugh McElhenny, Tommy Mason, Grady Alderman, Mick Tingelhoff, Jim Marshall, Bill Brown, Ed Sharockman and more. But the personification of the team for the six years he coached it was Van Brocklin. He engulfed the team and gave it its waterfront mentality. Vince Lombardi hated to play the Vikings. He had a football team with stars, discipline and championships, and in the early years Green Bay whipped the Vikings in all venues. But Lombardi was convinced that somehow Van Brocklin was schooling designated thugs on his team to maim his players. It was a suspicion that festered with special furies after Jerry Kramer, one of his best linemen, suffered a leg fracture in a game against Minnesota. None of the Vikings ever corroborated Lombardi's private charges in the years that followed. Which simply proves there are symptoms of paranoia in all coaches. Van Brocklin's last pregame orders to his brawling mediocrities were to "go get yourself a jockstrap," meaning "hit somebody." It's a code to which practically all football coaches subscribe. But it was heard with particular attention by the Viking warriors of the early '60s because not hitting somebody usually meant adios for the timid soul (if he was lucky) or consignment to the kickoff team (if he wasn't).

Van Brocklin dominated the field and the administrative offices and almost all of the personnel decisions and the conduct of the team. Because he did, the first years of the Vikings were routinely chaotic some days, successful against all odds on other days but somehow always in turmoil. Because he was Van Brocklin he built his ragamuffins to such a pitch of defiance that in their very first football game they beat the most renowned franchise in pro football, the Chicago Bears, 37-13. Because he was Van Brocklin he convinced himself that losing the next seven games was proof that half of his team was imbedded in some kind of conspiracy to make the coach look bad. Because he was Van Brocklin he ordered a full, three-hour scrimmage three days before the next-to-last game of the season, in the first week of December. The practice field at Midway Stadium in St. Paul was frozen. It was as uncompromising as steel. The players flailed each other and cursed each other and then they cursed Van Brocklin. The scrimmage ended in a savage feast of mutual cursing. Nobody talked in the locker room. If Van Brocklin showed up, he would have been disemboweled in five minutes.

He didn't show up. He was preoccupied in his office, cursing the players.

In this jovial atmosphere, the Vikings played the Rams in their last home game three days later.

The Vikings won easily. A week later, on a charter flight fresh from a three-touchdown hosing by the Chicago Bears, practically everybody got drunk. The little war vet, Jimmy Eason, the team's equipment man, tried to stay out of it. He'd lost a leg in combat but limped around doing what he had to and never talked about the war. Jimmy affected a gruff attitude in the locker room, but it was a façade and everybody knew it and all the players loved the guy. The Dutchman admired Jimmy's loyalty and the trust the players gave him, but the Dutchman was so tanked on that flight that he overturned Eason's dinner tray in his lap. Jimmy's offense was that he'd asked an old associate equipment man onto the plane as his guest. Seeing the food tray incident, Bill Bishop, one of true patriarchs of surly football players, went gorilla. He threatened to throw Van Brocklin off the plane and would have if he could see straight enough to find the handle on the emergency door.

This was football of another time, friend. Did it have soul? Well, not on a plane coming back from Chicago in the middle of December. But this was one smudgy face of the football I remember. It was hardly the only face. But having lived the experience, you don't easily forget, or want to, the Vikings of the early '60s.

The survivors of Van Brocklin's early camps have come to acquire the unbreakable bond of men who have shared the rack. It is the kind of togetherness that would be understood by the victims of the Spanish Inquisition. In the first year one of the late-round draft choices bugged out under cover of night after the second day. He knew that his escape would cost him his $1,000 signing bonus. That figure is correct. It tells you about the economics of medieval pro football. Nobody had an agent. You were lucky if they let you read the contract before signing. "Those guys who spent time in Van Brocklin's camps scoffed when you called it a bonus," one of the players said later. "They thought it was closer to a bribe to come to camp at all." Whatever they called it, the escapee who shunned the $1,000 bonus left a note. He renounced any claim to the money with this terse explanation:

"I'm clearing out. I choose life."

The team statisticians later declared a large and pleasant rookie lineman named Jim Hayes as the holder of the undisputed record for early resignations from Van Brocklin's lakeside purgatory at Bemidji. He was timed in 12 minutes from the opening whistle. A vet remembered it:

"It wasn't so much the violence of those workouts that got to the guys, although when you go through three straight days of full-pads scrimmaging twice a day, you know what it was like in the Crusades. That first day in camp, the linebackers were running backwards across the field, across and over, across and over, and it's real tough running backwards, and in those years they didn't have weight rooms and round-the-calendar conditioning. Most of these people came to camp out of shape. Van Brocklin howled about that. We'd go through a whole series of drills and calisthenics so that you were a sweating hog before you ever started hitting. A lot of people were wheezing and ready to barf. We were supposed to be in shape for it. To make it all legal, the doctors doing the medical exams came with electrocardiograms, x-rays, hammers, needles, forceps and the whole armory. Even in those years they were worried about liability.

"This big rookie tackle starts coming through the ropes on opening day and he goes through four times. He was all in a sweat and his eyes were getting bigger. On the fifth run through the ropes he did this half-gainer and flopped on the grass outside the ropes. His eyeballs rolled, and Fred Zamberletti, who was going to be the Viking trainer forever, looked really worried and ran over to the guy. Nobody knew who he was and nobody snickered, because nobody was feeling very fresh. Jimmy Eason came running with Fred. The tackle immediately recognized a friend in Jimmy but he was groaning and lying there exhausted and he says to Jimmy:

'Get me to the church, friend. I am going to die.'

"Jimmy had been in the big war, of course. For a while there I thought he was going to dig under the guy's jersey and shoulder pads to find his dog tag so he could get him to the right church. But Van Brocklin walks over about then. I'm not saying he was insensitive. But it wasn't like nowadays where if the same thing happened the coach would come over looking very solemn and alarmed and bring two doctors and a minister with him. Today you'd find the TV cameras coming in behind the coach and he'd look deep into the guy's eyes to let him know all that mattered to the coach, and the team, was this fellow's health because, well, football is just a game."

Van Brocklin never called football just a game, and he didn't know a whole lot of ministers. So the scenario didn't play out that way. The Dutchman crouched down and looked at the fallen knight with a reasonable show of concern. But right about then he decided that what the guy really needed wasn't spiritual comfort but a one-way flight out of Bemidji on the nearest North Central Airlines' DC-3. The Blue Goose. That's what they called the flight. Nobody is making this up. There was a Blue Goose that averaged 110 miles an hour on calm days. And the gasping tackle, having made a remarkable recovery, was on it the next day.

There were witnesses at the scene who truly believed that the prostrate rookie really believed he was either going to meet his maker or meet the devil. When he saw Van Brocklin, he must have been convinced that the maker was out to lunch and he'd gone the other way.

Not surprisingly, the stresses of Van Brocklin's camps occasionally stirred the inmates into some form of rebellion, the most popular of which was violating the 11 p.m. curfew.

It was always a mistake. It never did any good for their sympathizers to tell them in the cold light of reality that they should have known better. You'd figure they couldn't forget the demoralizing experience of one of their pals, who was stricken with loneliness in camp and got caught by a campus cop trying to smuggle his new girlfriend into the dorm. The cop let him off with a warning and, in an act of chivalry, kept the news from Van Brocklin. The amorous player was resourceful. He escorted his beloved into one of the nearby lots where he'd parked his car. As a love nest, it had some compensations. It offered less comfort than a couch but it did have more mobility. The trouble with this alternative plan was that resourceful lover forgot about the time. It got to be 1:30 a.m. The vacancy in the athlete's room was reported to Van Brocklin by the duty warden for the night, one of his assistant coaches.

Van Brocklin exploded and set off on a personal patrol of the parking lots. It took him only a few minutes to detect suspicious movements in the back seat of one of the cars. Peering inside, Van Brocklin found his missing half-back locked in the arms of amour.

Van Brocklin made no claims to being a psychologist or a sentimentalist. He was never very sympathetic when his athletes developed symptoms of horniness after hours. Unsentimentally, Van Brocklin reached through the open window and pried his stunned gladiator from the caressing arms of his partner. One moment they were joined in what the Victorian novelists called a compromising position, and the next they were abruptly unjoined. Van Brocklin had no interest in Victorian literature. His rule was simple: Nobody on this team screws around after curfew. He ordered the unhinged lover back to the dorm, ending a promising romance.

It was left for the last Sunday in camp that year for Van Brocklin to deliver his final retribution against the team's scofflaws. The Saturday night bed check at midnight revealed the absence of two of the wiliest, Bill Bishop and Charley Sumner, a defensive back. A third absentee was Raymond Hayes, a rookie fullback. Van Brocklin got the report and launched himself into the predictable rage. This time it was personal. At the week's last prac-tice he made a point of warning about any new offenses against order tranquility in camp. At 8 o'clock on Sunday morning he barged into Jimmy Eason's dormitory room. The Dutchman grabbed the foot of Eason's cot, collapsed the legs and spilled the startled occupant onto the floor. It was Van Brocklin's way of announcing the coach's arrival on business.

"Wassa matter, Norm?" Eason grumped. "It's Sunday. We don't have a team breakfast."

"We've got three bums who need an extra workout this morning," Van Brocklin said. "Get down to the locker room."

Jimmy made no further objection. He had a running start on a hangover. One look at Van Brocklin's red-streaked eyes told him that negotiations with the Dutchman were useless. Sumner, Bishop and Hayes appeared in the locker room a half hour later. Eason issued them full battle gear, includ-ing helmets, shoulder pads and blocking pads. From the locker room they walked the 400 yards to the practice field. There was foreboding in their hearts and a funereal pace to their walk, as though they were walking toward a loaded cannon.

They had it about right.

Van Brocklin was waiting for them in the middle of the field. The August sun was rising in the cloudless sky, pouring near 90-degree heat into the steaming grass. For Sunday strollers on the nearby parkways, it might have been an innocent sylvan scene. Birds chirped in the overhanging oaks. Squirrels romped, hunting for acorns. On another day it might have been a place for poets. But Keats didn't have to play the Bears six days later.

Van Brocklin met the trio at the goal line.

"All right," he said, "I want you to get down and do barrel rolls to the other goal line."

They rolled to the other goal line. Van Brocklin followed them.

"All right," he said, "I want you to roll back the other way, 100 yards." They rolled back 100 yards. The rolled back and forth, 100 yards at a time. And then they leapfrogged and somersaulted. Back and forth. Again. Back and forth. The sun got higher and hotter. Even when performed by a healthy man, these are unnatural acrobatics that will usually raise hell with the abdominal tracts. At this hour, Sumner, Bishop and Hayes were not healthy men. The night before at the Duchess Tavern, the Vikings' refuge from all the oppressions of training camp, had left their innards queasy and unpredictable. Nights at the Duchess had a tendency to do that. The Duchess looked like a stockade that could have been built during the French and Indian War. Wear and tear had knocked out the indoor plumbing. For relief the customers were directed to the mulberry jungle behind the tavern. Like every other bar in Minnesota, it theoretically closed at 1 a.m. But the Vikings were accorded special treatment as the unchallenged celebrities in town. It was at the Duchess where the once-fearsome defensive lineman from the Louisiana swamps and Baltimore Colts, Don Joyce, established a record that still stands in the annals of National Football League off-the-field performance. By the time he came to the Vikings, Joyce was girthy and aging. He was still a substantial figure, expanding by the month. Beginning at 2 a.m. after the team got back from an intrasquad scrimmage in Fargo, North Dakota, Joyce consumed 75 bottles of beer in a 24-hour span. He has never denied it, although being a man of innate modesty, he has never claimed credit. Purists on the team tried to take some of the edge off Joyce's feat by pointing out that some of the bottles were the 8-ouncers they called "splits." Joyce freely admitted the same. But somebody put a gold star in the Duchess' window in Joyce's honor. It was the Duchess' version of the Hall of Fame.

On that steamy and epic Sunday morning in Bemidji, nobody could tell you how many times Van Brocklin rolled Bishop, Sumner and Hayes up and down the field. After an hour one of them asked for time out. Van Brocklin ignored him. The temperature edged past 90. By now the rest of the team had heard about the bizarre melodrama taking place on the field. It was out of the pages of Dostoyevsky's *Crime and Punishment*. Scores of dormitory windows opened to the scene. Some of the onlookers crept up behind the oak trees. They made sure they stayed out of sight, because in his present mood Van Brocklin could easily have dragged them out to join the condemned three. They all understood that in those moods Van Brocklin could not be appeased, and that his furies went beyond impulsiveness and approached the pathological. In those moods Van Brocklin settled for nothing less than scorched earth.

The rollers got sick, naturally. The sicker they got the more contrite they sounded. "Dutch," one of them said, "take a thousand out of my pay but don't make me roll down that goddamned field one more time."

Van Brocklin dismissed the offer out of hand. "Roll down that goddamned field," he said, "one more time." With the hour of 11 a.m. approaching, Van Brocklin picked his way out of the messy field and left the three flattened players semiconscious at the 50-yard line.

There were no further curfew violations in camp.

"The first thing I want you to do when he comes to the line of scrimmage, no matter what the formation, is walk up there and hit him in the mouth."

–Van Brocklin instructing cornerback Earsell Mackbee how to deal with a sweet-talking receiver.

How Much of the Maiming Is Intentional?

*I*f a football coach today tries Van Brocklin's primitive company punishment of 40 years ago, he's going to wind up in criminal court and probably in handcuffs. He's also going to get sued for $10 million and fired on the spot.

All of this would happen on the same day, in time for the 6 o'clock news.

Nearly 40 years later it is a Monday night in September, which means millions of television sets are trained on professional football. Monday night pro football by now is a national festival, an honest-to-God celebration of the country's addiction to it. The game is preceded by two uninterrupted hours of hype and promotion on every available sports channel, including the ones that compete with the network broadcasting the Monday night games, ABC. It is the ultimate cross-pollination of the mercurial TV business of today: competing networks promoting each other to feed their mutual golden calf, pro football. This game is now more than king of the American sports culture. Pro football is its godhead. There is a scene on the TV screen on this night that rivets the viewers from ocean to ocean. A motionless player, Steve Young, is lying unconscious at midfield while a trainer and doctor attend. The coach stands near the player, crouching with his hands on his knees, silent and worried. And because of this scene, a question surfaces for one of the viewers (me). It leads to an interrogation of a football traditionalist (me).

"Here's one of the great players of modern football, laid out on the field with another concussion. He's still playing after his earlier concussions. He's not playing this game any more for the money. He's got enough of that. He's playing because it's in his blood. He's playing because he's hung up on competing. He's saying, 'I can still go, and I love the game. Don't carry me off this field. I can walk.' So he walks.

And all of these millionaire studs he's playing with and against seem genuinely awed by that. Is this guy tough, or what? Isn't he the same kind of ballplayer Hornung was talking about 40 years ago, the guy who goes to the wall?"

Of course he is. Young would have been a star and a committed football player in any generation.

"And in this same game, here's Bryant Young, the defensive lineman, same team, the 49ers. He's playing with a metal rod in his leg because a year before he fractured it so badly some doctors said he'd never play again. Here he is in 98-degree heat, playing in the Arizona desert. And late in the game, bushed and practically crawling, he sacks the quarterback to clinch it for his team. Could this guy have played for Hornung's team?"

Of course. He's that good and that tough. Plus Hornung would be the first to tell you that he and Bryant Young both played Notre Dame football, when it *was* Notre Dame football.

"So you admit that pro football players of today are just as hard-shelled as they were in those days you like to idealize."

I wouldn't call it an "admission." I don't know anybody who has watched pro football evolve over the last 50 years, and still finds it immensely absorbing, who would claim that today's players aren't as willful and as tough as the earlier ones. They're also bigger and faster and mostly better-conditioned, the exceptions being slobby nose tackles whose highly specialized art is based on being fat and able to occupy a space six yards wide without moving.

"So why all this lament over how football's changed? If the players are bigger and faster and just as tough, and if the coaches are just as smart or smarter, hasn't pro football found something better than it had in 1960?"

One of the things it definitely has found is the way to the bank. It has found a way to pay mediocre quarterbacks $5 million a year by making the citizens subsidize the quarterback. Pro football does this in most cities by letting the billionaire club owners extort tax money out of the citizens to build a new stadium that the owners could finance themselves if they marketed honestly.

"So how does that affect the team?"

It means the quarterback is gone in a year and they pay the next one, a first round draft choice, $7 million to learn how to play pro football.

"And what if it takes him five years to learn?"

They fire the coach, put in the West Coast offense and demand another stadium.

As a self-confessed traditionalist, I have no special interest in knocking today's pro football. As long as they can keep the quarterback and the running back out of traction for at least three games, it has moments of magnetic entertainment value. When you allow for all of the Cover 2 and zone blitz gobbledygook, the game is still recognizable and suspenseful. Sometimes it's worth three hours on TV, but the times when it's not are mounting. Why? The money stakes in winning and losing are now so huge the strategic risk-taking has gone south. The game often dissolves into a yawning struggle of field goals in which the soccer kickers–often the lowest-paid people on the field–overshadow the multimillion dollar quarterbacks. So for multitudes of fans today the saddest words are not the announcer's "that 60-yard pass *just* missed" but "that kick was wide right, again."

So today the most powerful and the fastest athletes in the game play defense. Directly or indirectly the team's defense often scores more than the team's offense, partly because the offensive stars are too maimed to play, knocked out for weeks at a time by fractures and concussions delivered by the supercharged defenses.

Many of the players–starting with Brett Favre and including Troy Aikman and Junior Seau, Cris Carter, Tony Boselli, Marshall Faulk, Terrell Davis, Tim Brown, and the pardonably wacky Warren Sapp–are as good as some of the Hall of Famers. There just isn't as much in the game today to, well, treasure. Granted, each play is still a war. That is the stylized description of football. It was in the older years, too. But now resurrect Norman Van Brocklin of the 1960s. Every play for Van Brocklin, of course, had to be a bitter-end brawl between our guy and their guy. Plant the bastard! It didn't matter in the 1960s that their guy usually did the planting. What Van Brocklin wanted was our guy to do more than plant the one across the line. Van Brocklin wanted absolute annihilation.

Van Brocklin's blunt dictum was to cream anything and everything that moved and it didn't matter where or how you did it. Hit somebody. Every ball club has some of this same violent philosophy. This is a brutal game. For all of the poetry of Jerry Rice leaping to catch touchdown pass in stride in the end zone, there is Steve Young lying senseless on the ground. Is it as true today as it was then? Yes, of course. Here is the Giants' Mike Strahan again, being interviewed in one more venue of the midweek *NFL Tonight* shows. Was it troubling what happened to Young? Yes. What would Strahan have done in a game in which the opposing quarterback is playing with a history of injury, bearing in mind that the quarterback could beat the Giants?

Mike Strahan said he wouldn't try to take him out for the season. But he *would* try to get him out of a game the Giants had to win.

This is the code. The game is for money. Do what you have to do to win. You don't want to paralyze the guy. But sometimes you do paralyze him. Strahan was talking about the difference between hitting with all of the velocity in his power (which might knock the player out of the game) and hitting with the actual intent to injure. There is a difference. But the laws of anatomy that govern the human body don't usually know the difference.

The code doesn't always produce grim results. Sometimes it delivers comedy. It tended to create more comedy in the macho theater of the Van Brocklin era. Understand, when your man hits a ball carrier near the sidelines, you call it aggressive football. When the other guy does it to your man, it's a cheap shot. Neither Van Brocklin, George Halas nor Vince Lombardi seemed to understand why the officials could not comprehend this simple truth. In the consensus judgment of the pro football clans of that era, nobody delivered more enthusiastic cheap shots than Bill Pellington of the Baltimore Colts of John Unitas' time. Very few people actually hated Pellington. Seeing him broadax an unwary halfback as the halfback eased up out of bounds was to watch a man happy in his work.

He did it to the Vikings' Tommy Mason one day in Baltimore. Mason recalled it years later from the sanctuary of retirement. "Pelly was a great ballplayer but one of the roughest, meanest characters I ever met on the field, although he was really a decent guy off it. We're playing this game in Baltimore and our fullback carried up the middle and I'm just sort of swiveling around trying to look alert when WHAM! Pellington bangs me crunch in the mouth with a forearm.

"I just looked at him dazed and then said something goony like, 'what the hell did you hit *ME* for?' It was one of the first games I played. When I got to the sidelines, Van Brocklin told me to get back in there and let Pellington have it. We were going to run a sweep and the Dutchman says, 'I want to see you throw a block on Pellington and tear his goddamn legs off at the roots.'

"I was lined up on the flank. Hugh McElhenny started a sweep to my side, and at the snap of the ball I came off the blocks like it's life-and-death. I angled straight for the middle of the field, and there's Pellington trying to ward off the block of our center, Bill Lapham, which, of course, he did. I was coming full tilt and I had him dead to rights. Just as I poured everything I had into the block, Pellington took one step backward and I crashed straight into Lapham.

"I damned near killed my own center. Lapham was reeling around when I looked up and the play was dead a few yards away. They just buried McElhenny on the sweep. I got back in the huddle and I figured I had to say something and I kind of croaked, 'who made the tackle?'

"McElhenny was rubbing blood from his nose across the back of his hand and he said, 'the meanest and ugliest bastard on the field. Pellington. Who the hell do you think?'"

Mason was spared Van Brocklin's retribution. Van Brocklin was occupied chewing out the woozy Lapham, who literally didn't know who hit him, Pellington, Mason or Van Brocklin.

The Dutchman admired prizefighters, particularly knockout punchers, and once contended that Rocky Marciano would have made the greatest strong side safety in the history of pro football. No pass receivers, blockers and wandering tight ends would be left standing, Van Brocklin said, if they came into "Rocky's House"–as today's ballplayers would describe it. Maybe Van Brocklin's admiration for people who threw haymakers had something to do with his own urges to throw punches. In the second year of Bemidji, Van Brocklin was drinking beer with some of the Viking owners at Jack's Bar when a well-oiled customer approached him at the bar and started taunting him. Van Brocklin tried to avoid any immediate outburst of violence. So he perfunctorily kicked the troublemaker in the shin and kneed him in the groin. Undiscouraged, the customer razzed him some more. Van Brocklin abandoned his strategy of passive resistance and swung a roundhouse right. The punch missed the customer and landed full in the gut of Bernie Ridder, one of the Viking owners. Ridder was a big guy who liked Van Brocklin and harbored a streak of mischief. "Dutch," he said, "I won't ask for an apology. I've been hit harder in a crowded elevator."

If that disclaimer was supposed to give Van Brocklin peace of mind, it didn't. He thought the punch he threw was a pretty good lick. A year later, walking out of a supper club in Birmingham, Alabama, the night before an exhibition game, Van Brocklin was accosted by a Dallas sportswriter, who was one of throngs of sportswriters Van Brocklin called gutless, frauds and imposters. The writer asked a question about Tarkenton. The question seemed within the parameters of his job to get some news. Van Brocklin snarled. The reporter asked the question again and Van Brocklin swung a right. The reporter had more mobility than Van Brocklin figured. He ducked and Van Brocklin's fist landed squarely on one of the building's stone columns.

Van Brocklin held a news conference from his hotel bed early the next morning. The purpose was to explain to nosy Twin Cities journalists why he was wearing a large bandage covering his right hand from his fingertips to his wrist. I got there late and asked Roger Rosenblum of the St. Paul newspaper what was the Dutchman's explanation. Roger shook his head. "As far as I can make it out," he said, "the Dutchman is claiming that he was the victim of unprovoked attack by a pillar."

Which meant that Earsell Mackbee, a young defensive back from California, should not have been startled by the orders he got from Van Brocklin before a Vikings' game with Baltimore early in the season. Mackbee ultimately became a fashion statement, walking the sidelines in a full boa when he was on injured reserve with one of Bud Grant's early teams. Grant had limited enthusiasm for boas. It need hardly be noted that Mackbee did not walk Grant's sidelines, or draw a salary, very long. But he acquired a deserved reputation as a tough guy in the Van Brocklin years. "I got my big chance to break into the lineup in the Baltimore game," Earsell remembers. "I had to cover Jimmy Orr, a really fast and nifty receiver who had all the moves. I'd played a lot in the San Francisco game the week before. In that game George Rose started on the left corner and Bernie Casey caught three touchdown balls over him. Van Brocklin sent me in there, and to prove it was no fluke, Casey caught a touchdown ball over me, too. The funny thing was, and I'll never forget it, at halftime there was George Rose coming up and telling me things about how I could play it better. There was a lot of racism in pro ball then. But here was George Rose, a white guy from the South, telling me things about how to play—and I was trying to take his job.

"We won that game in San Francisco 42-41 but this was the next week and here was Orr. Van Brocklin told me before the game, 'I know exactly what Orr is going to do. He's going to try to psyche you out right off the bat. Don't listen to his frigging sweet talk. The first thing I want you do when he comes to the line of scrimmage, no matter what the formation, is walk up there and hit him in the mouth.'

"That's what he said. I didn't give it another thought. Hit this guy in the mouth? Here I am, a rookie. I just couldn't picture myself going up to this nice guy, and that's what he was, and doing that. For that particular game they had an article about me in the program. A lot of players read the program in the locker room before the game to kill time. Evidently Orr read it. When we lined up for the first play, he says very politely, 'pretty nice article about you in the program.' And I said, 'hey, thanks.' And then he said, 'how are the wife and kids?' And I said, 'fine.' Now you tell me how I'm going to hit this nice sociable guy in the mouth when he's never done one bad thing to me? The game started and he put the moves on me. The one that really hurt was right near the end of the half, when Gary Cuozzo threw 50 or 60 yards and Orr scored on me.

"Van Brocklin didn't say a word about me not following directions. But you got to know that this guy would never forget. We didn't play the Colts until the next year. Orr didn't start but he came in during the first half. I decided this is it. So on the first play I gave him a forearm to the face, which was legal then. He kicked at me, and I took after him. We started rolling on the ground, and big Jim Parker of the Colts came over and took off his helmet and was planning to clobber me, and both benches cleared. Before you know it's a free-for-all and then it gets to be practically a riot. Orr and I both got thrown out. He said something as we were leaving. I couldn't make it out, but I know sure as hell it wasn't about the wife and kids."

Earsell knew one other thing. It was one way to stay in Van Brocklin's starting lineup.

Advocates of peace and reconciliation are almost certain to be appalled by these random revelations of life in the National Football League, especially of life in the menagerie Van Brocklin assembled.

Mackbee was surprised that the Dutchman didn't issue cans of Mace to his athletes before the kickoff.

So I'll concede that ballplayers of 40 years ago didn't have any better manners than the muggers of today. The difference might be that in 1960 a guy was willing to play when he was dazed from a butt in the head. He was allowed to stay in the game, in the words of one coach of the time, because a lot of players in those years played in a daze most of the time. It was not the most chivalrous way to describe those more primitive times. But that's the way they talked and coached and played.

And nobody worried about lawsuits.

"Palmer, honey, here's your lasagna."

–Marie Pyle, daughter of Mafia figure Tough Tony Accardo,
pouring steamy hot pasta on her husband's bare torso
in bed after he stood her up for a Viking party.

A Jilted Lady Strikes with a Boiling Lasagna

*M*ost of the sins of today's football are forgivable. The zealous pursuit of money is not an original vice. But mention the name of Palmer Pyle, and I will give you one indictment that pro football 2000 can't dodge.

The game today has largely outgrown the authentic screwballs it once sheltered. This means the unchained spirit of Palmer Pyle of the 1960s' Minnesota Vikings is now hopelessly orphaned and there will be no more like him to resuscitate pro football's vanished society of instinctive wackos.

For this, I want you to join me in mourning.

Palmer entered the National Football League as the son-in-law of one of the infamous godfathers of the Chicago underworld. Before he left he was nearly roasted alive in the fumes of a steaming lasagna delivered by his gorgeous and highly indignant wife. Regrettably, there are no post-season awards for football players who barely escaped incineration by a platter of lasagna. Others have received recognition for risking less.

Which doesn't mean today's pros are more polished human beings than their forebears of 40 years ago. If you pay any attention to the grotesque end zone exhibitions that today are palmed off as the impetuous celebrations of youth, you know better. And, yes, there are people in the NFL today who are accepted eccentrics. Shannon Sharpe of the Broncos blabs unstoppably and takes the vows of silence in alternate years. Johnny Randle of the Vikings is a high-octane gabber and locker-room clown and Warren Sapp of the Buccaneers announces his invincibility before every game. The problem is that all of these people play football at relatively high levels of performance. Palmer didn't and was never intimidated by the opportunities to do it. Plus, he was that rarest of football flakes, a man with a creative genius for producing turmoil. He did it unconsciously. Nobody did it better, including the immortal Johnny Blood, who once hung by his fingernails on the outside ledge of an eighth story hotel window to escape a Packer coach prowling the hotel at midnight to locate curfew violators.

Palmer joined the Minnesota Vikings from the Colts in 1964, already having acquired some notoriety as the son-in-law of the Chicago Mafia's Tough Tony Accardo. Pyle left the Vikings the next year, his professional life about to go south and his marital life in even worse shape.

As a confessed apologist for the game's Dark Ages, I concede that pro ball demands from today's athletes–spare me for this–more "athleticism." Right there let me ask for forgiveness. I thought we could get through at least one dissection of the phenomenon of pro football without getting burned by that horrendously overcooked chestnut of the football panel shows, "athleticism." I have been beaten down into a near-coma by the word "athleticism," battered beyond the point of further resistance. Hasn't everybody? We now fully expect Jaws Jaworski, Sterling Sharpe, Mark Malone, Tom Jackson and even Marty Schottenheimer, for heaven's sake, to glorify somebody's "athleticism" three times a night. And, of course, they have now infected their listeners. Americans who are otherwise known to talk sensibly find themselves using "athleticism" in casual conversation. "Athleticism" surrounds us and suffocates us and when I hear it I want to scream. Chalk up one more moral victory for the saturation of America by today's TV-speak. It's made neurotics of us all. And if this plea for mercy is beginning to annoy you, I have a question. "How did we survive the previous 75 years of pro football without knowing about this mystical quality: that when a player jumps to catch a ball, runs fast or is adroit enough to avoid being beheaded, it means he has 'athleticism'?"

I now leave the confessional. Thanks for your tolerance. I'll also stipulate that Palmer Pyle never had athleticism.

Palmer was a football player, all right. He was formally designated as an offensive lineman with the Minnesota Vikings. But his great contribution to the ongoing saga of pro football in America was his originality as an inspired flake. I can't blame the football brain trusts of today for not granting refuge on their rosters to a man of Palmer's spacey wanderlust. I would probably do the same. The reaction of today's general manager to a Palmer Pyle would be a sudden and panicky urge to protect the franchise at all costs. If the budget could handle it, he'd probably want to launch Palmer to the moon, which is where some of his pals thought he originated. To this, as an old confidante of Palmer's, I can only enter a loud objection and say there is sometimes too high a price for peace and quiet.

Palmer was a Michigan State man who came into the National Football League as a guard on the offensive line. He came with chubby red cheeks, a broad chest and sturdy buttocks. He had no conception of rational behavior. He had a brother playing center for the Bears, Mike, who was a Yale man and a pillar of orthodoxy.

One of his off-field running mates remembers Palmer this way:

"When he came to the Vikings from the Baltimore Colts he already had a reputation for being one of the all-time ding-a-lings, although he was pretty great to be around. He was a squat kind of guy with this puffy face and a deep baritone voice perfect for telling stories. Nothing shook the guy—coaches, general managers, defensive tackles, cops or his wife, Marie. He sort of set the stage at the Viking welcome home luncheon before the season. We won big in the exhibition games. The interviewer at the team luncheon asked Palmer, the new man we got from Baltimore, what he thought was the reason for the Vikings' success. He said, 'I think it was the shrewdness of their off-season trades.' While Palmer was in Baltimore he once hid a turtle in the foot of Jim Parker's bed. Parker was one of the gentlest guys you ever saw off the field, but he was one of the toughest, strongest linemen in pro football history. On this night he'd read about some guy getting killed by a snake down South. It was the goofiest coincidence. Pyle had slipped into Parker's room a little before and planted this turtle under the sheets. Parker was reading this story about the snake to his roommate. Just as Parker got to the climax of the story, the turtle moved and nudged up to Parker's foot.

"Well, Parker came out of that bed roaring like Vesuvius. He headed for the door, and if it hadn't been open he would have taken out the whole wall. If he knew Pyle was the guy, he would have squashed him.

"There was a story going around in camp that the reason Palmer got in bad with the Colts before being traded to us was that he talked back to Carroll Rosenbloom [the owner] and Don Shula [the coach]. Palmer was a guard. He said, 'if you switch Jim Parker from tackle to guard [which would have knocked Palmer out of job], I'm going to have my father-in-law come down here with two cement vests, one for each one of you.'

"The guy was one of the all-time roamers. He would take off and have a few schnapps and you didn't know if you'd see him again. He invited a lot of people over one Thanksgiving and was the only one who didn't show up. He went out to get the cranberries and just didn't come back for two days.

"I'll never forget the time Bill Jobko, one of our linebackers, and his wife Katie were going to have some of the players over for a lasagna party. It was right after a game and everybody was supposed to go home and change into something casual. Palmer was the only one in the group who forgot to go home and pick up his wife. Marie was really a peach, but she had an awful temper.

"Marie went home after the game and got herself all prepared and waited for Palmer to come back to take her to the Jobkos' place.

"My wife and I were about the last to leave the party, and that was the last I saw of Palmer that night. He seemed to have a great time, and we all figured that Marie decided not to come. Palmer liked the lasagna so much he took a whole tray that was left over and made himself a big martini, and headed out of the Jobkos' apartment to his own. We saw him sort of stumbling through the parking lot. The rest of it we heard from Palmer later. He got home and knocked on the door and she opened it. Palmer said, 'you should have been at the party, hon. It was great.' There she was, waiting for him for hours, dressed to the nines, and the guy says 'you should have been there.'

"This teed her off something fierce, as you can imagine. So Palmer goes into the kitchen and puts the lasagna in the oven and turns it up piping hot. He then goes into the bedroom and strips down and is lying there like King Tut, and he yells, 'hey, Marie, when that lasagna is done, bring it over here.'

"He's still sipping on his martini waiting for the arrival of his devoted wife with the lasagna, but she's out there waiting for the mess to get really steaming hot.

"After 15 more minutes she takes it out and brings it into the bedroom and says, 'Palmer, honey, here's your lasagna.' And she dumps the whole thing on his chest. The guy nearly went up in flames. He roars out of bed and starts throwing that hot cheese and goop in her hair, and I guess it was the wildest scene in the history of the suburbs. We got the story more or less that way direct from the returning hero. Everybody in the locker room used to rush the door when Palmer came in to get the latest news from the arena, like you call the newspaper when you want the late baseball results.

"He was with us for just one year, but I kid you not, with the ones who knew him, he's still one of those inside legends. When the Vikings finally got to the Super Bowl six years later, some of the guys wanted to vote him a quarter share just to keep him in lasagna if nothing else. It didn't exactly shock us that Palmer was among the missing when the Vikings put together their roster the next year. The guy was really unbelievable. I remember him telling me about another spat he had with his wife in the off-season, when he had a projectionist's job but he preferred to spend most of the time at home resting up for the great adventures of the next training camp. They lived in one of the north Chicago suburbs. Palmer sometimes occupied the winter hours feeding the birds and protecting the home from squirrels with his BB gun. She got a little weary of that and hid the BB gun.

"He came home one night when Marie was out of the house and couldn't find the BB gun. He scoured the place and finally located it and stationed himself in one of the easy chairs. Using his best sharpshooting form with the BB gun, he picked off every one of her family portraits on the wall. Ping, ping, ping. Just like that. One glass-covered relative at a time."

There is no public record of Marie Pyle's response when she got home. We do know that Palmer was able to get through the winter without going into traction, which he had to claim as a moral victory.

"He decided not to bother showing up for the last day of practice," his confidante said. "Palmer had a suspicion he was going to be traded. It might have gone back to the week before, when we played the Giants. The Vikings were having a big day at Yankee Stadium in December and some guys on the bench got into a yule log mood. It was really cold. Everybody was wearing those big Afghanistan warm-up coats, but it wasn't enough for Pyle. He talked Jerry Reichow, who was then one of our receivers, into helping him build a little tent out of their warm-up coats behind the bench. The next thing we knew, somebody on the bench yelled, 'my gawd—Palmer's on fire!'

"Which he was. Palmer had built a little fire in the tent and was warming himself around the hearth when the flames starting running up his coat. It took three guys to save Pyle from being incinerated. He could have been the first NFL ballplayer to get cremated wearing hip pads and a face mask."

It hardly has to be mentioned that one unsympathetic witness to Pyle's thermal performance was Norman Van Brocklin.

"Naturally, Palmer was gone the next year. I can't say I especially blame the Vikings. But they would have shown me a little more class if they retired the guy's number."

It may have been that Palmer's behavior was foreshadowed that summer in training camp when Reichow, Paul Flatley and Roy Winston rented a boat for a Sunday afternoon's fishing on the Mississippi River. Palmer was blameless. His spirit might have been there but his body was at the Duchess Tavern, protecting Palmer from the ravages of thirst. The team had returned that morning from an exhibition game in Atlanta, where the humidity loused up Reichow's Iowa-fed respiratory system. He sneezed all the way back and still had not fully recovered when they boarded the boat. In midstream, Reichow sneezed again. This was followed by a distinctive "*plop*" in the water a few feet from the boat.

"It has to be a walleye," Flatley yelled.

"Walleye, shit," Reichow muttered through pursed lips. "It's my teeth. They went over the side when I sneezed."

The water was murky. None of the mariners considered diving for the submerged dentures. Reichow braved the next four days on what his buddies described as "gums alone" until a replacement plate arrived from his homestead in the cornfields.

If the Palmer Pyles of those years belonged in the circus, Conrad Dobler belonged in a kennel. Dobler acquired notoriety in the 1970s as a genuine rabies menace on the line of scrimmage before the officials unpiled the bodies. Dobler played on the offensive line for the St. Louis Cardinals. The Vikings' Doug Sutherland came to me after the game one day, looking as though he had just fought off a vampire. "Listen," he said. "This guy bites. He did it to me four times. I'm lying there under the pile and Dobler clamps his teeth above my ankle. It hurt like hell. After the third time I told him I was going to come out for the next series wearing catcher's shin guards. I would have but the equipment guy didn't have a pair." Dobler never denied the charges. He snarled, "Tell Sutherland to stop worrying unless he needs a transfusion."

Did these uncanny events happen more often in the wilderness years of pro football than they do now? Possibly not. The difference might be that today they get smothered by the latest corporate battles between the ball clubs and the agents. In those years they acquired the homely status of folklore, for which thank God. There is no evidence, though, Palmer Pyle ever met Booth Lustig. If he didn't it was a gross injustice by the fates of the zodiac. Palmer and Booth were contemporaries. Booth had flawless qualifications to belong in the same zone of outer space with Palmer. Booth was a field goal kicker with the Pittsburgh Steelers. He was willing and earnest but not particularly accurate. The Steeler archives are filled with stories of Booth's unworldly problems kicking the football, some of which defied the laws of gravity. Booth kicked when the goal posts were on the goal line, 10 yards closer than they are today. Despite this he was said to be the only field goal kicker who kicked one ball that flew over the line of scrimmage and then ducked under the goal posts in a mysterious knuckleball action never before witnessed in an NFL arena. He practiced on the sideline by kicking empty beer cups, many of which flew further than his field goals. In one game he kicked a ball straight into the exposed duff of Ray Mansfield, the center. In another, he missed the ball and kicked the knuckles of Dick Hoak, the holder. Against Buffalo he flubbed a late field goal attempt that probably cost the Steelers the game. Hounded by guilt after the game, he refused to join the team on the flight home, took his bags, went out on the highway and hitched a ride.

These accounts can be documented.

They can never, however, be logically explained.

"Wouldn't pro football be a beautiful game if everyone played it the way Hugh McElhenny does?"

—Inscription on a plaque given to the veteran runner by the Chicago football writers before a Vikings-Bears game.

McElhenny and Lawrence Taylor Build a Bridge

*L*awrence Taylor was inducted into pro football's Hall of Fame in 1999. Hugh McElhenny, who for two years gave Minnesota audiences an unforgettable flashback of his greatness, got there years earlier. They played the game a generation apart and, in style and temperament, they might have sprung from different planets.

One lived on violence on the football field, the other on finesse and a genius for escape. One, Lawrence Taylor, played and lived like a man hounded by personal and game-day demons within. McElhenny, on the other hand, dealt with life and homicidal enemy linemen with a kind of wry realism and streaks of amusement. Life largely was OK and probably generous as long as the tight end finished the block and got him around the corner.

They were two memorable football players, with personalities that could never harmonize. But there was a linkage between them that unmistakably identifies a quality in the great athletes. It bridges the generations, revealed by a timeless imprint to their performance that may explain the game's appeal across the decades despite its radical changes.

And what was that quality?

Hugh McElhenny was a running back. Almost no one has brought to that calling the same art and bravura that identified his game. They lifted his open field running to the edge of the concert hall. Somebody said it was the closest approach he's ever seen to ballet on the pro football field. It may have been. But if you're going to mix dance with pro football, you'd better make that a pretty hairy ballet and remember that McElhenny never ran back a punt in little red shoes and tights. Whatever football's episodes of grace, it's still a brute game, and McElhenny never forgot that. He was a sociable and relaxed guy away from football, and even managed to transmit those qualities to the field. When I knew him, in his seasons with the Vikings, he was past 30 and playing on his reserves of craft and his dwindling aura. His face, toasted olive by the California sun, was lightly creased in an agreeable way that made it the portrait of a jaunty man of battle. Most of the dominos in his life looked to be order. Playing football gave him a stage in tune with a carefully controlled ego that didn't need postures and fury to lift him out of the crowd.

Lawrence Taylor was a linebacker who seemed to live and to play football in an unrelieved attitude of simmering wrath and hostility. In his public demeanor and often in his behavior he had the look and sound of a man fueled by hatred and resentment, almost pathologically so, bristling at a world that seemed to him determined not to understand Lawrence Taylor.

Yet nobody in pro football's more than 75 years played linebacker with a more stunning blend of speed, bolts of power, creativity and raw, terrifying disruptiveness than this man.

So we ought to explore them together, these two emotional opposites whose gifts made them players who belong to the football ages but who confronted Sunday afternoon with utterly different character and psyche. You've seen Lawrence Taylor and the few contemporaries who matched his impact. You may not have seen McElhenny. If not, accept my sincere regrets. If you were honestly stirred by the end-to-end ferocity and domination with which Lawrence Taylor played football, you would have been captivated by McElhenny's fluid skills and guile. The question is, what was it that connected these two extraordinary football players beyond their prints on the game they played? Something that defines the star quality they shared.

A TV man with a microphone, groping for some credible ideas, posed that question to me not long ago. He thought I was a logical guy, and he gave a reason. I was, he said, one of those old lions of the newspaper jungles who might know something he missed. He may have been right about the old lion business. If so the lion's claws were now a little more fragile and his teeth a lot longer. What the man was asking me to do was to dissolve the time warps. He wanted me to compare the pro football game then (McElhenny's time) and now (Lawrence Taylor's time and beyond). I said the first thing is to avoid any generational gridlock and I could do that by admitting my age. It's possible you didn't hear the Joe Louis-Max

Schmeling heavyweight title fight on the radio in the 1930s or watch the demise of the Hindenburg dirigible in the *Movietone News*. I heard and saw these things. I don't make that claim with any vanity. It is simple evidence that I have outlasted enough wrong-headed editors, epidemics, wars and vengeful jocks to have watched and written pro football since the time it was emerging from the caves. This does not give me any special football wisdom beyond what millions of television watchers exercise every Sunday afternoon from the sanctuaries of their living rooms. There they are supreme in their hindsight in addition to their insight. It's the same place where I watch most of my football today. An option is to drive to the Metrodome in Minneapolis to watch it on the scene. The thought of doing that gets more hideous each year.

I admit that watching it in the stadium, the Metrodome, does give me a renewed intimacy with the game that is not quite matched by listening to Pat Summerall's amiable mumblings on TV. That is the theory. But each time I'm tempted to revisit the stadium atmosphere of my earlier times, any stadium of the earlier times, I remind myself that these are not the atmospheres of the earlier times. I can go to the Metrodome today and pay parking fees and concession stand prices that invite bankruptcy courts. When I walk into the arena I can yearn for the old voltages I felt from the crowd but what I get are supercharged amplifying systems that threaten me with brain death. I enjoy the energy and the feel of the game I often get in the arena. But more often what I get today is prolonged numbness in all of my extremities caused by a wild man who looks like Jesse Ventura with hair, charging around the field on a motorcycle. There are other hazards. If I do go to the stadium, and I decline to scream and howl to unhinge the Green Bay offense in the red zone, I'm seen by the screamers around me as a moron, a suspected recluse or a saboteur.

When we look at football's time warp, we have to start out on common ground. Technically and from the standpoint of conditioning and sophisticated strategies and player resources, the game today is easily a superior product. This is not the same as saying it is more appealing or more entertaining. A lot of the time it seems more tiresome, and *is* more tiresome, simply because of its nonstop exposure. The pregames and post games, the chain reaction replays, kickoff at noon, kickoff at 3:15, kickoff at 7:15 and again tomorrow at 8. The head whirls. Which game is this, 49ers today or 49ers on *Memorable Moments* from 1981? Is it live action or replay? Allow time for the medics to carry a player off the field on a cart. Did somebody say the game today is more dangerous? It is, but that was inevitable in spite of the Star Wars equipment of today. The bodies today are bigger. They move faster. Which means the velocity at impact is higher. Every play, every player is on view on somebody's TV. So there's a higher premium on making an impact, which means putting somebody's cranium or sternum–and sometimes his very life–at higher risk.

You need only to walk through the high-tech training rooms of today's football team to understand the level of physical conditioning in today's football. I hadn't visited the Vikings' training quarters at Winter Park in the Twin Cities for several years until last September. And here was a vast armory of conditioning machines, row on row, in use not only August to January but February to July. If you don't train the year-round in pro football today, it's adios. See you on the waiver wire. In the days of the caves, the players drank beer or worked second jobs to keep the repossession agents away. Half of them came to camp flabby. The only flabby people on view in today's football are the ones whose job specifications require them to be flabby, or at least to weigh 340 pounds, which usually amounts to the same thing.

When you think about it, that's a ghastly weight. The American Society of Cardiologists ought to come out against it. But the cardiologists are probably watching just as hysterically from the same Sunday afternoon sanctuaries as everybody else. So the game keeps getting bigger and better, with faster runners, more neurotic coaches and bigger guts. It keeps getting richer and more popular and more violent and risky and yet even more alluring (often to me as well as you) and only God or Jaws Jaworski knows where it's headed.

But because you may be too young to know about the Palmer Pyles and Dutch Van Brocklins, I'm offering these vignettes out of the crannies of a modest memory to give you some idea where all of this came from–all of the dazzlement and melodrama you see on Sunday from 10 a.m. to 11 p.m. It may be a little grand to call it football's heritage, but that's what it is. If you watch the show today you're entitled to know what you missed in the yesterdays. It's why the man with the microphone wanted to know about the connection, those times with these times, and I said you could find it by looking at Taylor of the Giants and McElhenny of the 49ers, Vikings, Giants and Lions.

They connect the game because they played with a charismatic quality that put them beyond imitation. They were originals who played with such intuitive craft and rhythm (McElhenny) or such overwhelming assault (Taylor) that their performances eluded the accepted markers of excellence of the era in which they played. Their styles put a signature to pro football in a way that resisted emulation, so much so that audiences of any generation could recognize them as unique–the one unchangeable measure of greatness.

Linebackers don't need statistics to achieve that rare status. Taylor above all didn't need them. Running backs usually do, and McElhenny didn't have numbers on the astronomical scale of the Jim Browns and Walter Paytons. Nor would he displace Brown and Payton at the head of the usual lists of all-time runners. But we're not necessarily talking about the "greatest" runner or linebacker. We're talking about a one-of-a-kind with the skills or speed or power to elevate them above their peers and to ignite the galleries. Players like that cut through the calendars: Sammy Baugh, Don Hutson, John Unitas, Dick Butkus, Jerry Rice, Joe Montana, Brown, Payton and Gale Sayers, Mean Joe Greene, Jack Tatum, others.

Hugh McElhenny and Lawrence Taylor.

So here is Lawrence Taylor entering the Hall of Fame. Some said he shouldn't because he kept getting hooked on drugs after he finished playing, that he had a police rap sheet that ran out onto the sidewalk and a lifestyle filled with gold earrings.

All of which may be true but does nothing to deny him what he deserves as a football player.

What he did was to resculpture the position of linebacker, simply and absolutely and irreversibly. He turned linebacking from a role into a commando mission. The mission was to destroy the opposing team's offense. This was not exactly a new concept for football defenses. But Lawrence Taylor's concept owed nothing to the old schemes. Taylor believed it was possible for one man to destroy an offense.

And he would do that. He was everywhere. He lined up over here or over there. He lined up on the defensive flanks and in the middle. Often he switched in the midst of the play, disguising his assaults. Wherever he went, the offense tried to surround him or simply to slow him or, even more simply, to run away from him. The rules of the game sometimes made this impractical. The offense, after all, was limited in its flight by the sidelines. He wrecked offenses by terrorizing the quarterbacks, by sacking them or sending them to the hospital. If he felt any remorse for this kind of behavior it was not evident on the line of scrimmage on the next play or in his interviews with herds of spellbound reporters in the years to come.

So how could this man possibly find common ground with a Hugh McElhenny, who as a running back was dependent on his wits and nerve and his instincts and was constitutionally opposed to random violence on the football field?

The answer from McElhenny, the realist, would be "Thank God I didn't have to be on the same ground with that guy."

He did usually outrun or survive other carnivorous characters like Ray Nitschke, Bill George, Big Daddy Lipscomb, Gino Marchetti and Andy Robustelli.

In a typically obnoxious December gale in Chicago (add freezing rain), McElhenny was invited to midfield before that game by the head of the Chicago football writers. He'd been exiled to the first-year Minnesota Vikings after nine years with the San Francisco 49ers in the coach's unseemly act of retaliation for a couple of fumbles. In San Francisco, they called Hugh "King." King of the Halfbacks. The people who called him that were the players, who don't express homage very often. The Chicago writers presented him with a plaque. They did it quickly because they wanted to haul their duffs back to the press box, where George Halas had grudgingly allowed some heat to be piped in. Not a whole lot, because Halas hated to spend any needless nickels in any venue, particularly one where he was the emperor. The Chicago writers, nonetheless, were in earnest. They'd watched McElhenny come into town for years and run those sweeps or off-tackle cuts, and weave and swerve through the mastodons and outwit the linebackers, and turn 2 yards into 20. They had admired him for all those years and they weren't bashful.

"Wouldn't pro football be a beautiful game," their plaque read, "if everyone played it the way Hugh McElhenny does?"

It was such a generous tribute that it needed a postscript. McElhenny might have recognized his obligation to respond. It didn't take long. Ten minutes into the first quarter, he caught a Bears' punt on his 19-yard line, dodged the first wave of the coverage, deked another and swept up the middle of the field, veering right without changing stride and coasting into the end zone. To one of the press box beagles he seemed dangerously oblivious of a massive Bear charging after him.

"I did catch sight of the guy when I looked back for the pursuit," the King acknowledged. "He was wearing a number in the 70s. Even after running 60 yards, an old guy like me, I figured there's no way a guy wearing a 70 is going catch up with me."

When you depend on your brains as well as your wheels to avoid dismemberment in pro football, you don't miss much.

A player of McElhenny's time could not possibly have engraved himself into the national football consciousness in the way that a Joe Montana or a Barry Sanders, John Elway, Reggie White or Deion Sanders did years later. Pro football of that time was not the bombshell presence on television that it is today. There were no TV highlights around the clock in those years. In today's hothouse television marketing, you could be totally ignorant about pro football, couldn't tell a red dog from a hot dog, and still recognize Dan Marino's face instantly because he's selling somebody's high fashion leather gloves on TV every year at Christmas.

In those years they didn't use the word "panache" to characterize that special stamp on a player's performance that set him apart, the verve and aplomb with which he played. McElhenny had it running with a football in the same way Zorro had it with a sword. I always thought a McElhenny performance bore a kinship to the opera house as much as the football field. His kind of football took him beyond the spectators' partisanship. When he played on the road, the crowds in New York, Washington, Detroit and Chicago never seemed especially offended by the ineptness of their defenses when one of McElhenny's runs left their heroes lurching and panting. Privately, they had to admit admiration. If you looked at football as an orchestration, McElhenny was the soloist. A fan whose team lost to the Packers' power or the Cowboys' passing game might have found scapegoats among the miserable clowns on his own team. But McElhenny rarely left them with any anger. Years later Michael Jordan aroused the same kind of response on a much grander scale, of course, because Michael was a world figure and an icon of the masses beyond all icons.

The best of McElhenny's runs were irresistible drama. None of it, however, was done for show. He dipped a shoulder here, offered a limp leg and then withdrew it from the lunging tackler. He changed speeds and almost never gave the defense a frontal target. He was an intuitive runner, but it wasn't all instinct. His high school coach had taught him about leverage. "Where the head goes, the body has to follow," he said. So McElhenny would recycle the lost craft of the stiff-arm, jamming his hand against the tackler's helmet. "You could often turn him away from you by using his own weight and charge against him. You could throw a hip into a tackler and pull it away, and just walk away from the tackle. Most of that was reflex. Some of it, I have to tell you, was just fright."

But not much. He threw his skills and technique against the maulers. He was the whirling, high-stepping cavalier defying the onrushing macers. Until Barry Sanders revived it in the 1990s, he was one of the last of a breed, the halfbacks who saw the field as a tapestry and read the texture on the fly. McElhenny was taller and a little more gymnastic than Barry, who flitted and darted and practically made himself invisible. If you had to take McElhenny out of the concert hall, put him in the bull ring. He was the matador, feinting and gliding in the middle of all the snorting and the serious chance of dismemberment he was facing. His last such performance was on a sunny October day at Metropolitan Stadium in Minnesota when McElhenny reached back into his prime for a valedictory run that represented one of the last echoes of a grand career.

The Vikings played the 49ers, McElhenny's paymasters for nine years. The Vikings had reached the 49er 32. McElhenny swung left behind two pulling guards, dipped back slightly to give them room to block and started to turn the corner. The guards disappeared somewhere in the scrimmage. McElhenny dodged the cornerback and then the linebacker. He slanted toward the center of the field. Linemen hit him at the hips and shoulders but they didn't hit him very hard because he was twisting and veering and he looked like a man threading a minefield. Matt Hazeltine, a linebacker and McElhenny's insurance broker in California, grabbed at him and missed. So did another linebacker and the safety. McElhenny crossed the field again. It was beginning to look like a graveyard of fallen bodies, none of them McElhenny's. By actual count on the film later, seven 49ers hit him or tried to. Near the goal line, Hazeltine overtook him and drew another bead on him.

The King pulled his shoulder in. Hazeltine flew by and missed him again. With the end zone underfoot, McElhenny lifted his knees slightly and pranced in, with the one pardonable piece of showmanship to which the great ones are entitled.

McElhenny was brave enough when he had to be. But one of the joys of watching him play and talking football with him was to see in this marvelous and pragmatic athlete a total absence of poses. His professional philosophy was the code of the escapist. He never construed football as a game where he had to establish his enduring manliness on every play. He expressed it offhand in the daily repartee of the Viking locker room at old Midway Stadium in St. Paul. George Shaw, the quarterback, brought up his recollections of his days with the Baltimore Colts.

"A guy who was really dedicated to football," Shaw said, "was Dick Syzmanski. He was a bachelor then. He told me he'd actually lie awake nights trying to figure out new ways to hit people."

McElhenny winced and allowed himself a moment to reflect on this violent philosophy.

"Me," he said. "If I were going to lie awake nights, I'd spend them trying to figure out ways to *avoid* getting hit."

McElhenny could not have spent many sleepless nights. Avoiding destruction was something he did naturally, and oh, so memorably.

"Mercer, you couldn't kick
a whore off a piss pot."

–Norm Van Brocklin giving a field goal kicker
a somewhat inelegant evaluation of his accuracy.

A Hard Man to Love on Sunday Afternoon

*T*he only sound that gave Van Brocklin any peace on Monday mornings after his misfits lost a football game was the voice of Ray Charles singing one of the torch ballads that made millions of folks misty in the '60s.

The only places near Minneapolis where Ray Charles was available on Monday mornings were the jukeboxes of the blue collar 3.2 beer joints in suburbs like St. Louis Park. Van Brocklin would telephone me around 10 o'clock in the morning.

He rarely introduced himself. "You still writing about that lousy football game?" he asked.

"It's Monday morning," I said. "It's already in the paper."

"Yeah, I read. Every golden syllable. How the hell do you make a turkey like that sound like a football game? I'm ashamed of the way we played."

"The readers already know that," I said. "You said it on three different pages in the newspaper. I thought your team was respectable, Coach. You play Green Bay and lose by only three touchdowns. They're better than you at every position. I don't know how you could have played them much better. Lombardi said as much after the game."

Van Brocklin almost gagged. "The goddamned spaghetti-eater. He had us by the nuts and he knew it. I couldn't believe how he sucked us in on that play pass. Did you see it?"

This was standard Monday morning dialogue between the coach and the journalist. Van Brocklin didn't want to replay the game. He wasn't looking for reinforcement. He wanted to exorcise something that boiled inside him after each loss. What he wanted was to get out of the house or the office or wherever he spent Monday mornings, and listen to Ray Charles.

I said I was at the stadium Sunday and managed to notice the play he brought up. It was basic football. Bart Starr faked a handoff to Jim Taylor into the line. The Vikings mobbed Taylor. Starr turned, still holding the ball and threw 50 yards downfield to Boyd Dowler. It's called a play action pass. Eventually even the best defensive backs get burned by it.

"Dowler is just standing waiting for the football to come down," Van Brocklin groaned, "and our guy [Rich Mostardi, the safety] is still looking into the backfield 20 yards away. He has no idea where the ball is or where Dowler is."

I could imagine the royal chewing-out facing Mostardi when they did the films. I thought somebody ought to lobby for him. "It was a good fake by Starr," I said. "I was fooled myself."

The Dutchman's mood suddenly changed. He sounded delighted to hear the news, his suspicions confirmed. "Oh, that's beautiful," he said. "That qualifies you to write pro football."

The Dutchman's snarls had receded. He was giggling over his punchlines. What he needed in these day-after sparring sessions was an excuse to be sociable again. He usually followed with a gruff invitation to listen to Ray Charles. We drove around, found a place and ordered Cokes. Van Brocklin got some quarters and fed the jukebox. Ray Charles started singing "I Can't Stop Loving You." It was wistful and moody but, for Van Brocklin, oddly healing. I thought, here was the voice of a blind man coming out of a machine in a gloomy beer parlor in the middle of the morning. His sound and art were guileless, easy and personal. They seemed to spread some form of solace over this pathologically competitive man festering from the loss of a football game that was not exactly going to change the course of the world. The scene, I thought, was slightly comic: Ray Charles' therapy parlor at 10 in the morning. The Dutchman took a few moments to drift into a reverie. "Isn't this guy great?" he asked. I nodded. How could anybody not respond to the songs of Ray Charles? To validate this opinion, Van Brocklin played "I Can't Stop Loving You" six times in the next hour. For a change of pace, he asked me what I liked from Ray Charles. I said, "Try 'Georgia.' Georgia On My Mind." Van Brocklin played "Georgia" six times.

We talked football on and on. It was all off the record. The only other customers in the tavern were two guys wearing denim work jackets drinking beer at the bar. In the year 2000 on Monday morning they would be yammering about the Vikings game. But this was 1961. They talked for an hour about the weather. In another culture an eavesdropper would have been floored by this performance. It was nonstop gabbing about the weather, fixing the furnace, greasing the snowblowers, trading in the snowmobile for a new model next month, bitching about not getting off for the deer season, backtracking to the worst wind-chill in St. Louis Park last January. Why would the eavesdropper be surprised? This was Minnesota. Delirium over pro football and baseball did not come suddenly or naturally in Minnesota, where watching the ice form on Lake Minnetonka is still an important spectator sport. In 1991 three hours after the Twins beat Atlanta in the final game of the World Series, a fan in the suburbs driving around honking his horn to celebrate was arrested for disturbing the peace.

If it were today the two barflies would recognize the Viking coach the minute he walked through the door. Two days later the town would be wired with rumors of the Minnesota Vikings head coach spending all Monday morning drinking beer in a bar. You could predict the aftermath. TV camera crews would stake out the tavern. The bartender would be an instant celebrity, interviewed for every news show in the Twin Cities plus *Sports Center* on ESPN and Fox. But this was 1961. The guys at the bar didn't recognize the coach. They would have ignored him if they did.

For most of my years of association with Van Brocklin, we got along with some rough version of mutual respect. Those attitudes were often interrupted by long sieges of mutual antagonism and once by a near fistfight in Detroit. A neutral would probably say we had the kind of combative personalities that were bound to collide. They did. The long interludes of frigid silence that followed were usually more damaging to me than to Van Brocklin, because he was the one and only authority on the team. And if I didn't quote Van Brocklin during the week somebody on the newspaper, then the *Minneapolis Tribune*, was certain to do it, leaving me to gnaw on my misguided sense of honor. The somebody was usually my occasional pal, Sid Hartman. Sid is the indestructible Minneapolis sports columnist who went so far back in time that the guys on the sports desk had this story about Sid: He once interviewed Hiawatha with the idea of bringing big league sports to the Twin Cities. According to the sports desk, the deal was that Sid wanted to talk Hiawatha into backing a public bond issue to build a retractable dome over Minnehaha Falls and make it a theme park.

We worked for the same newspaper but were competitors in ways that only we cared to understand. I found Sid to be a man with normal stores of love in his heart but with the compassion of a barracuda when he found a colleague disabled by his source's grudges.

So the battles and frail truces with Van Brocklin never ended. I decided early if it was going to be a fight, the battlefield ought to be level. I said if we started calling names we might as well hang it up. Van Brocklin said he didn't have to resort to calling names. I said that was wonderful and I was willing to be fair about it even when our arguments hit the red line. Van Brocklin sneered hearing that. "Fair about it," he said. "Is that what you call being a horse's ass?"

We laughed a lot in those honky-tonks. I was never quite sure what motivated our sessions and I'm deadly certain that no managing editor would condone them today. Maybe it's what Van Brocklin needed to quell the rages inside him. He was a brainy guy in a violent business, to which he contributed more than his share of violence. When he was calmer and the talk got around to college football he would confess, without boasting about it, that he needed only three years to earn a degree at the University of Oregon. But turmoil was at the core of his professional environment, and if the day was short on turmoil he managed to concoct some. Creative as he was with his strategies and impulses, as a football coach he was a horror show for any self-respecting psychologist. He was vile and abusive with his players, sardonic and just plain domineering. His ethnic slurs were proverbial. He talked privately about some of the African-American players, but not all, in language that today would be considered abominable, and was abominable then.

In this he was hardly alone. In his racism he was no better nor worse than most. On the field he was impartial enough. He would often rail against the lack of heroism (his view) of a black halfback like Bobby Reed. But he would do the same of a white quarterback like George Shaw. He was a football creature of his time and his culture. Words like "nigger" and "black asses" were a common part of the conversation currency in the coaching lingo of those years, which didn't make them any more forgivable. Some coaches didn't use them. Lombardi and Tom Landry didn't. Don Shula didn't. There were others. When Van Brocklin sometimes brought them into our conversations, I didn't deliver lectures. Piety doesn't usually wear well in the macho societies. Sometimes I just walked away. What I should have done was to write it before I eventually did. But those conversations *were* private. Under the rules of engagement they were handled as such by most if not all of the people in my business. If one is allowed retrospect, what would have stopped it quickly would have been the presence of black reporters on the scene. There were none. The newspaper personnel departments in those years weren't any more magnanimous in racial attitudes than the coaches. There are African-American writers and coaches today, and the racial issue–while still capable of erupting–is being resolved. Looking backward, when you say the racial drift of many football coaches of 30 and 40 years ago reflected the society of the time, it leaves you with only one available truth. God, the abuse we so casually inflicted on people.

The Dutchman was the best quarterback in pro football when he retired in 1961 after winning the league championship for Philadelphia. His notoriety as a hard, ramrod guy in his leadership and his rhetoric made him an obvious choice for somebody's head coach. It wasn't going to be in Philadelphia, since he had already slandered most of the management there. The Vikings' first general manager, Bert Rose, applauded gleefully when that happened. Recruiting Van Brocklin as the Vikings' coach was going to be Bert's passage to glory as a brilliant administrator and choreographer. For a year or so it was. After which Dutch began maneuvering Bert's departure, which didn't take long.

That was the Dutchman: They were going to do his agendas. His way, every day. He could get this done. Get the pencil-pushers the hell out of the way.

The pencil-pushers were anybody with decision-making power in the organization's office. They may have played or coached, but if they didn't play or coach today he didn't listen to them. He didn't listen to Joe Thomas, the team's early scouting director, or to Rose. He made an exception of the team's early business manager, Billy Bye, a former University of Minnesota football star. And eventually he did listen to one of them, Jim Finks, who succeeded Rose as the general manager. Finks had quarterbacked in the NFL. He had coached in the United States and Canada and had been a general manager in Canada. Beyond this, he was a guy of decency and perception. He also brought with him common sense and integrity in all of his dealings in the NFL, which later produced the trades and draft choices that lifted Minnesota into the Super Bowl four times. Anyone who worked with him would have to be a fool not to recognize those qualities and a total sociopath to reject his friendship or his counsel. Van Brocklin was neither of those. Finks was his friend from the day he arrived in 1964. He humored the Dutchman when that seemed right, calmed him here and there and stayed away from the football field. In ways that football men understand, he let Van Brocklin know that Jim Finks was no threat to him and had no interest in second-guessing him. Van Brocklin trusted him from Day 1. It was one of the few professional and personal relationships in football with which Van Brocklin felt an absolute comfort. If he'd lived, the Dutchman could not have been surprised to see Jim Finks himself voted into the Hall of Fame.

So the Dutchman was no one-dimensional ogre, which we can talk about in a few minutes. But he coached in an attitude of constant wrath and was hounded by the suspicion that most of his football players were malingerers, unsalvageable mediocrities or just plain dumb. He actually had more players of quality in his early years in Minnesota and later Atlanta than he was willing to admit to himself. Tarkenton was already a star in his rookie season. Van Brocklin's highest redeeming quality as a coach was an ability to lift players of limited skills to a playing level beyond those skills. He was a creature of will, impulse, intellect and ego. His greatest virtue as a competitor was his unbreakable belief in himself. It pushed him to rare levels of performance under duress as a player. When it rubbed off on his teammates or players, it did same for them. When it spilled into impatience and frustration, it pushed him into spasms of cruelty and vindictiveness.

He had a positive genius for spontaneous fury and a bewildering hit list of villains in his private or professional life. He would usually call them phonies, as in phony newspapermen, phony general managers, phony Notre Damers (not to be confused with phony Big Tenners) and phony All-Americans in the player draft. He spoke emotionally about the bedrock values of loyalty, pride, family devotion and personal discipline. But he had a hard time crediting the men who played under him or against him with the same. When he valved off most of his tensions he was a merry and needling leprechaun in the locker room or in the lounges. In those moments he was an appealing sort of guy. His fondness for the old days of the NFL was profound and almost tender. But it also acted as a dividing line in his mind between his list of phonies and "the real ones," the achievers, the regular guys. These were usually players from the South, with whom he identified more easily than the others, although he was born in South Dakota and grew up in California. His wisecracking off-the-field impishness and his generosity made hundreds of friends. His reputation as a winner and as a quality coach on the sidelines was deserved. So was his reputation to be able to will marginal players–or intimidate them–into the attitudes of winners. He was at his best in the roughhousing of the evening chugalugs or the yarn-telling sessions with football people, up to and including football people from the newspapers. Ultimately he alienated many of the people who called him their friend. With the Dutchman, you were with him 100 percent, all the time, or you didn't belong and couldn't be trusted. In other words, you accommodated to his whims and his wraths or you were a phony. So a lot of those friends and a lot of his players wound up telling him to go to hell.

His tongue was tart, inventive and memorable. Nobody could puncture a bumbling football player with Van Brocklin's originality and his four-letter eloquence. In their first year the Vikings employed a field goal kicker, Mike Mercer, who was one of the nomads of his time in college and pro football. He attended four or five different colleges, with his kicking tee and resumes in hand. For a variety of reasons, his tenure at all of them was brief. He was a likeable enough guy but moved about with the wariness of a man worried about getting hit by a passing freight train. It didn't matter that there were no railroad tracks in sight. Field goal kickers tend to paranoia. Mercer usually wore a crew cut that gave him the appearance of a German infantryman about to hit the trenches. He had a strong but erratic leg. He would kick field goals from 47 yards out but miss them from 20. He did this not once but twice in a game at Metropolitan Stadium. The second time, sensing a torrent of vitriol from Van Brocklin, Mercer shunned the direct route to the bench and made a long loop around the cheerleaders in the hope that Van Brocklin was occupied with somebody else's bumblings. His strategy had no chance of working. Van Brocklin didn't wait for Mercer. He pursued him. He yanked off Mike's helmet and gave him a terse evaluation of his work.

"Mercer," he screamed, "you couldn't kick a whore off a piss pot."

Mike heard this novel judgment in silence. If he laughed he would have been fired. If he applauded Van Brocklin's punchy rhetoric he would have been fired. If he argued he would have been fired. So he kept his mouth shut.

And, of course, he was fired.

Van Brocklin's gift for invective followed him geographically. When he left Philadelphia he made an unprovoked assessment of the Eagles' future: "This team was nothing when I got here and it'll be nothing when I'm gone." His prediction was not exactly soaked with modesty, he admitted. But it did have the virtue of being accurate. When he was about to leave as the Atlanta coach years later, he offered a personal scouting report. He said his team would have won more games if the players spent more time concentrating on football and less time with the whores of Peach Street. This was headline news all over Atlanta. It did nothing to improve the comfort zones of the Falcons' wives, but it did speed the Dutchman's departure.

Van Brocklin's assessments of the world around him were versatile. He was a student of military history and, not surprisingly, admired the style of Gen. George Patton. He also dabbled in political science, a curiosity that may have been the source of his answer to a reporter's question after Garo Yepremian, the soccer kicker from the Mediterranean, beat his team with six field goals. "How do you stop that?" the reporter asked.

"Change the immigration laws," Van Brocklin said.

I'm not sure that line was an original. I do know that Van Brocklin claimed credit for it. Who wouldn't?

You could look at this tumultuous personality, Van Brocklin's, and regret the absence of some grace and balance in it, something to make it more agreeable over the long haul. But that's a flip judgment, not quite fair. Van Brocklin sometimes brought his workaday tempests home with him, but he also brought a familial love that was constant. His wife, Gloria, was his partner, confessor and his champion. His daughters adored him, with reason. With them he was a generous and demonstrative man, as he was with two Asian youngsters he and his wife adopted in later years.

His openhandedness with people in trouble seemed instinctive. In the off-season of the Vikings' third year of operation, the team's business manager, Billy Bye, encountered the Dutchman in the hallway of the team's offices. They did the usual how-are-you scene. The two of them hit it off well but the Dutchman seemed troubled. "Jim Marshall and some of the other guys are having money troubles, Double B," he said. "I'm hearing that and I want to talk to him. He's got to get it in gear, and I mean that. He's coming in today. I've got to lay the lumber to him and I'm going to do it today."

Nobody was paid any boxcar salaries is those years. Marshall clearly was going to be a star, but he needed a loan from the club now and then and was accommodated. Van Brocklin liked him, of course. Anybody who didn't like Marshall had to be a candidate for the shrinks. He was full of bounce and the exuberance of being a football player. He spread that special kind of gusto wherever he went. It seemed to embrace the world, his teammates, the ball club's employees and once in a while even his creditors. He was a little loose about handling money. A few hours after Van Brocklin's declaration of all hell to pay, Marshall walked into the Viking offices immersed in his vast fur coat and wide-brimmed black hat.

He greeted Bye and all the secretaries in the office. Almost immediately, the place glowed. Any Marshall entrance affected the atmospherics that way. Bye motioned him to his desk. "James," Billy said, "the Dutchman wants to see you. He's mad. You probably know what it's all about. Better go in there now, and all I can say is be ready." Marshall walked down the hallway and knocked on Van Brocklin's open door with the usual million dollar smile.

"The door slammed and nearly caved in the rest of the building," Bye remembered. "The Dutchman was taking no prisoners."

More than an hour later Marshall walked out of the building and Van Brocklin came striding down the hall. "How did it go?" Bye asked. "It got taken care of," Van Brocklin said. Bye looked inquisitive. Van Brocklin stared at him. "I said I handled it. It's over."

Bye was prudent. He decided on silence. So he just stood there, inviting a reasonable conclusion to the day's saga.

"Look, Double B," Van Brocklin said. "We talked a long time. You know, the guy really does have some problems."

"So what did you do?"

"I gave him 500 bucks. I told you it got handled."

The Dutchman never thought much about proprieties, although you'd never call this fellow any kind of social Bolshevik. In mixed company he was a charmer and something of a gallant. But he pictured himself as "a surface guy," without airs or shifting faces. What you saw, in other words, was what you got. If something felt right to him, he'd say, it *was* right. If a guy like John Wayne had that figured out why can't everybody else? Why let the hairsplitters run the world?

In the midst of a newspaper strike he offered me a loan of several thousand dollars. I thanked him and explained why it would be impossible for me to accept. I brought up the conflict it would or could create, the ethics problem and all of that.

Van Brocklin tried to look at this argument thoughtfully but gave that up as a hopeless act.

"Conflict, my foot," he said. "Whether you took it or not I'd still expect you to be as pig-headed as usual. That's your style. You're pig-headed. You've got the franchise."

Well, he may have been right. I didn't take the loan and not long afterward Van Brocklin saw me talking to Bert Rose, the general manager, in the lobby of the Sheraton-Cadillac in Detroit the night before a Vikings-Lions game. He made some animated motions to me suggesting he wanted to talk. Rose and I parted after awhile and I joined Van Brocklin. He'd sipped a few, maybe a few more than I had, but it was close.

"Why the hell do you keep talking to that guy?" he wanted to know.

I said Rose was the team's general manager. It was not unheard of for a football writer to talk to the chief administrator of the football club.

"He's on his way out. You want to know something about this football team, you talk to me." When the Dutchman got hot or drunk, or both, his eyes took on streaks of red lightning, which formed a nice compositional contrast with his flashing teeth. I said something to the effect that the coach's wisdom was always welcome and something to be treasured. The Dutchman didn't think this sounded very sincere. "You're gutless," he said. "You're like every writer I ever met." I said something to the effect that the Dutchman was full of crap. He just went crazy. He said it was time to go outside and settle it. I said he was nuts. I told him that wouldn't do either one of us much good, probably me less than him because the Dutchman stood 6-2, almost a half foot more than I did. He yelled some more and said I was gutless. I said, OK, have it your way. Where do you want to go? He reconsidered the site of the forthcoming battle of the century. He said his room was better. He didn't want a scene in the Detroit newspapers. I asked what about the Minneapolis newspaper? It was the one, after all, in which I'd sworn to print all the news fit to print.

Van Brocklin said that if I wrote the story I was more gutless than he thought.

We took an elevator and walked into his room. We stood there staring at each other. I mean, how do two grown men start a fight over the general manager of a football team. Van Brocklin finally threw an unsteady right meant to land somewhere on the back of my head. I stepped inside of it, feeling dumb but ready to laugh. We clinched, fell on the bed together and rolled into the TV set, fracturing it in a million pieces.

Honor was preserved. Three hours later, at 4 in the morning, I got a phone call from Van Brocklin. The Dutchman had been around newspapermen all his adult life but knew nothing about deadlines. He thought there was still an outside chance I might be wrapping up a big expose on the fight. He invited me to his room for breakfast. "When?" I asked. He said now. I told him I wasn't writing about the fight. "It's a non-story," I said. I told him I won on points because he was going to pay for the TV set, which, incidentally, he never did because the food service guy covered for him. The hotel food service brought in two monster platters of scrambled eggs, sausage and a six-pack of beer. At 4 a.m.! I ate some of the eggs. We talked about the Lions. Believe it. The coach of an NFL team is up at 4 a.m. the day of the game talking about how he's going to ambush the other guys, who happened to be the second-best team in football behind Green Bay.

I dozed for a few minutes in the middle of his monologue and went back to my room. I have no idea what happened to the beer. Eight hours later Van Brocklin's team played its best game of the season and came within one penalty of beating the Detroit Lions in their own house.

We didn't talk for three weeks. It was a break for both parties.

Was that a chaotic relationship? It probably couldn't happen today. The relationships then—reporter and coach, reporter and players—were fundamentally different. In most of the cities, even the large metropolitan cities, one newspaper, one reporter, covered the team. Mal Florence in Los Angeles, Sam Blair in Washington, George Puscas in Detroit, Cooper Rollow for one paper and Brent Musburger for another in Chicago. Roger Rosenblum was the Viking reporter for the St. Paul newspaper. Roger was a large, amiable human being and a great traveling companion who prided himself on being civilized in his tastes. We'd talk opera and the stage for hours. One of the rewards of being a Renaissance man, Roger felt, was being able to drink gin fizzes at the bar of the Jack Tar hotel in San Francisco at 9 in the morning on Sundays. Roger had huge stamina for these things and I don't think they affected his professional acuity at all later in the day. It didn't help his chances for promotion, though, when his newspaper's owner, Bernie Ridder, also one of the Viking directors, observed Roger in the hotel bar one Sunday morning at 9 a.m. Roger's been gone for years and I still mourn his death. And I suppose I also mourn what you could call the death of the times. In today's football, the media conferences after a practice are duly described as massive. Our version of massive media conferences in those years was Roger's considerable bulk arrayed beside my lesser frame in the little blockhouse Van Brocklin called his office at Midway Stadium—next to the Jimmy Jingle truck that fed Van Brocklin's troops at lunch.

All of this meant that a solitary reporter, prowling the practice field daily, had a professional football team practically as a private preserve. Once a week, maybe for 10 minutes or so on a Friday afternoon, a local TV station would show up with a camera. After the practices I'd kick field goals with a Jim Christopherson or Freddie Cox or stand in the pass-catching line at the end of practice for one of Tarkenton's throws. It was that informal. A little nutty, when you think about it today. So one day Van Brocklin, sounding waggish and conspiratorial, told the other coaches he was going to find out if I knew anything about catching a football. The coaches usually called me "Barney." The title was bestowed by Van Brocklin. It was a reachback to the era of Barney Oldfield, the automobile racer. Van Brocklin thought I drove a car like a man inviting a wreck. "Barney," he said, "Go down five yards and run an arrow." The arrow was what most people call a slant pattern, in which the receiver goes downfield a few yards and then cuts crossfield. Van Brocklin was not far removed from his championship years as an NFL quarterback. His arm was still one of the most powerful in football although he almost never displayed it in the Viking workouts, refusing to grandstand. But he thought this day might be a good one to come out of retirement. He told me how many strides to make before looking for the ball. I have to give him credit for that much chivalry. "On 3," he said. He barked the cadence. Hut. Hut. Hut. I came off the line in my wing-tip shoes and my polo shirt and broke crossfield. After the fifth stride I looked up, and the ball hit me in the gut. What it did, in fact, was to knock me down. It hit so hard it all but rearranged my insides. Before it did, I pulled my arms around it. This was no athletic move. It was pure, self-preservative reflex. I went down and held on to the ball. The Dutchman's coaches applauded. They didn't applaud too loudly because they weren't sure Van Brocklin approved the scene all that much.

He did, though. The Dutchman's guffaws bounced off the seats of the homely little stadium. He came over. "You did well," he said. "You can catch. You could play for this team if you had any brains."

I told him if I had any brains I'd give the job to somebody else.

The men he played with and against remain awed to this day by the ferocity, the unbreakable will and the skills with which he played quarterback. Of his coaching years they get philosophical. Some great players can make it as coaches, some can't. Some have the balanced personalities and patience to make it, some don't. Most of them consigned Van Brocklin to the second category, and the record probably concurs. Neither in Minnesota or Atlanta, though, was he actually evicted. From start to finish in football, from the Los Angeles Rams to the Philadelphia Eagles, to coaching in Minnesota and Atlanta he pretty much decided when he was going to hit the road. His teams in Minnesota and Atlanta were fundamentally works in project. In Minnesota he achieved faster than he had any right to achieve when, in the team's fourth season, it erupted with a rollicking offense behind Tarkenton and became one of the best teams in football. But a year later it lost dismally to Baltimore in a midseason game. Van Brocklin quit in exasperation. Jim Finks talked him out of it and he returned three days later to finish the season and the next one. But his effectiveness as a coach was dead, and not for the superficial reason assigned to it. The fans said the team dismissed him as "a quitter," for all his reputation for playing with guts-and-all. It really wasn't that. Van Brocklin led by intimidation beside his brains. He goaded and insulted and threatened. All of that could push young players faster and further than somebody else could. But when he pushed too far and too often, the Van Brocklin qualities that ignited his players eventually alienated them, and he became a caricature in the locker room. They laughed rather than feared. When that happens, the coach is finished. And he probably understood that, both in Minnesota and Atlanta.

With his demons, Van Brocklin wasn't going to stay very long wherever he went, and he probably wasn't going to win over the long haul as a coach. I'm not sure that made him a failure as a coach. It made him Van Brocklin. And how did a player read Van Brocklin?

Paul Flatley was a wide receiver for Van Brocklin for five seasons. He might not have been a typical Van Brocklin player. The Dutchman didn't scare him particularly. Flatley was a *bon vivant* night creature out of Northwestern, a good-looking guy to whom playing professional football was not necessarily the grail of his life. Running downfield he scarcely caused a ripple in the air. For foot speed he graded out slow, moderately slow and embarrassingly slow. But he was clever and resourceful and usually smarter than the defensive back covering him. He had to be, because in least a half dozen games he played with a howling hangover. That included a game in San Francisco in 1964 when he got back to the hotel at 8 a.m. the day of the game, somehow avoiding detection as a curfew violator. The equipment manager, Jimmy Eason, spotted him in the locker room and was appalled. "You look awful," Eason said. "If the Dutchman sees you like that, you're dead meat. Lay low."

He did, propping himself up with some blocking dummies he found behind the lockers. Eason poured black coffee into him for nearly an hour. Flatley played the whole game inspired by dread. What drove him was the fear that Van Brocklin would spot something askew in his pass routes. It was a circus of a game. The Vikings came from miles behind. Tarkenton threw eight times to Flatley. One ball was uncatchable. The seven others Flatley pulled in, twice sliding on his face and once fighting off three defenders in the end zone. He piled up more than 200 yards and two touchdowns and the Vikings won 42-41.

Eason almost had a stroke when it was over.

"You would come in and sit in on Van Brocklin's first playbook session," Flatley said years later, "and get the feeling that this man knows so much football you could never possibly get on to half of it. It wasn't just what he did with the X's and O's but the way. . . well, what the hell, whoever heard of a guy practically declaring war when he shows you how to execute a simple dive play?

"When he did give you a game plan later, he presented it like a hard-boiled salesman would. I've been in sales a good part of my life after football. I know that every good salesman has to exhibit confidence if you're going to believe him. This guy gave you the game plan in a way that made you believe that everything on that list was ready to work. The other team always did exactly what he said it would. And when this happened game after game, whether we won or not, you knew that this man wasn't grab-bagging to find something that would work. He had talent and brains even if he was so damned abusive to guys, and if you did what you were sup-posed to do it was going to be successful. He treated me OK but he said things to other players, publicly, in front of the squad, that were pretty awful. I disliked him for that because some of those people were my friends and didn't deserve it.

"The thing about this guy and his strong personality was that he was just going to run the show. Nobody else better try. Some of the rookies would come in really naïve or impressionable and were just overawed by the guy. Other guys, and I was one of them, would just let it run off their backs–just take him as a BSer with all that Captain Bligh attitude and rough language. I don't mean he was putting on a performance. I just mean that he never realized that some people would really take all that stuff as though it was the end of the world."

Maybe it's what Van Brocklin needed, some laughs in the film rooms. There were never enough of them. Ridicule? Too much of that. In a newspaper-man's career, the days of Van Brocklin were too vivid to forget or, in fact, to rationalize or sanitize. I never completely figured out our Monday mornings with Ray Charles. Maybe he wanted to grind his axes by privately ripping the players he didn't like in ways that he wanted to avoid in his coaching meetings. He liked to confide some of his schemes for next Sunday. Maybe there was some therapy in it for him. He was also doing some fishing. He wanted to know what his players were saying about him in the locker room. He never put it that bluntly but that was the idea. I usually laughed off those little expeditions and told him if he wanted a mole he could get one at the zoo.

For 10 years after he left the Vikings, we didn't exchange a word. Somebody told him about a remark I made about him, which was miles away from what I actually said, both in tone and substance. He called, screamed and shouted, and hung up. He didn't ask for an explanation and I didn't think I had to give one.

When the Dutchman died in Georgia of a massive brain hemorrhage in the 1980s, Gloria asked me if I would be one of the speakers at his service outside their home south of Atlanta. In my little eulogy I said that for all of his storms in football, he was capable of kindness and a real humanity. When a family asked for a football for a sick kid he'd bring the squad together and produce an autographed ball in five minutes. He offered money to old pros who were broke or drunk. He gave his roof and love to kids from halfway around the world and when he finally left football he did it his way, snorting defiance and refusing to compromise. He came from a time when the coach was an autocrat. The players could be roustabouts and they might be hung over on Sunday but they sucked it up and played. Much of that went out with the wind at about the time he discovered there was no place in football for Norm Van Brocklin.

He was often wrong-headed and too often unfair. But he was real; he left a mark on the game he played and on his times, and he was an original. I've always missed our good times. And there are days, driving through St. Louis Park, when I can still hear Ray Charles' beautifully raspy torch songs.

"It wasn't [a] bad [chewing-out] by the Dutchman's standards. He said it was the kind of chowderhead call you'd expect from a quarterback just out of nursery school."

–Fran Tarkenton, in the aftermath of a game in which he handed off to his fumbling fullback with 20 seconds left, costing the Vikings the game.

When the Vikings Shredded the Musicians at Wrigley

Most of the games in professional sports today are played in pleasure palaces built largely with money fleeced from the tax-paying public. The Pharaohs of the Egyptian dynasties would have admired the club owners' strategies, which are basically a modern version of the mugging schemes the Pharaohs used on the masses 4,000 years ago.

The difference was that in the Sahara Desert the public hauled 20-ton blocks of rock to build pyramids for the Pharaohs. In the U.S.A., the public pays extortion money to build stadiums for billionaire owners. It does this so that the billionaires who forced them to build the palaces can pay the millionaire athletes who play in them. In return, the public gets to watch its favorite millionaires play for a few years, before the fortune-hunting athletes find another billionaire with a stadium that pays more.

I'll confess that it's hard for me to love these gleaming new jock coliseums despite all of their aesthetics of exploding scoreboards, Hard Rock Cafes and waterfalls. It isn't so much the shakedown of the public that bothers me. If the taxpayers or the legislatures want to submit to it, they're welcome to it. Maybe what I'm missing is the old citizens' musical band in Wrigley Field in Chicago. Yes, they still play baseball in Wrigley. They still have vines and Sammy Sosa hitting home runs on the wings of the 30 mile an hour Chicago gales and people sitting on their roofs watching the action. But the Bears don't play football there anymore. I grant that Soldier Field, where the Bears do play, isn't much younger than Wrigley. But if the peoples' band still plays there, I don't hear it when I watch the Vikings-Bears at Soldier Field. And when I go to Wrigley for a baseball game today, I see Sammy just dimly. What I see with total clarity is the ghost of The Most Excruciating Football Game the Vikings Ever Played, and I see

Charley Ferguson, long legs, helmet, football and all, crashing into the citizens' band. And a few minutes later I'm looking on in disbelief as Francis Tarkenton, 20 seconds from winning the game, is *handing off* to the fullback. And the fullback is going down. And he doesn't have the ball. And less than 20 seconds later—

I'm not sure you can handle what happened at Wrigley that day in one gulp. We'll take it in charitable doses. My theory is that the quality of pro football's arenas in those years made some of their bizarre events inevitable and, when I look at them from this distance, practically immortal. They even shaped the behavior of some of the players and coaches. I give you old Forbes Field in Pittsburgh. The Pittsburgh Steelers played at Forbes. They were then coached by Buddy Parker, a canny but vile-tempered despot who once put the entire football team on waivers after an especially galling defeat. The Steeler front office wailed in unison, fearful it was going to lose half of its team. The fears were groundless. The Steelers were so bad that all of them—36 strong—went unclaimed.

The Steelers were an organization which for years resisted such new-fangled movements as the draft of college players, 30 years after it was instituted. By the 1960s, most teams arrived for the draft meetings with footlockers full of scouting evaluations. The Steeler front office arrived with five or six 3 by 5-inch recipe cards containing the amassed fruits of its research.

In the early 1960s, a group of the more zealous Steeler fans kept a small ceremonial cannon just off the corner of the end zone. It was their custom to fire the cannon and a blast of smoke whenever the Steelers scored. One of the Steelers' better receivers in that era was Buddy Dial, a slender Texan who was a reliable and steady player. Late in the game he caught a touchdown pass in full stride near the corner of the end zone. As he did, the cannon roared 3 feet in front of him, belching geysers of white smoke. Startled and half-convinced that he was shot, Dial leaped in the air and came down clutching for his delicate parts to see if they were all there. They were, but his teammates insisted years later that Dial was never the same player after that.

The fans at old Briggs (later called Tiger) Stadium in Detroit displayed even fewer symptoms of rationality than the cannon crew at Forbes. The Viking center at the time, Mick Tingelhoff, remembers coming out for the second half on a raw and dark December afternoon in Detroit. The wind smacked him in the face. It was a miserable day, unredeemed by the sun or the level of football on the field. It was uniformly lousy, perpetrated by two teams headed nowhere in the standings. Snow flurries spiraled out of the upper decks. "I looked around the stadium," Tingelhoff said, "and I couldn't figure out what was going on. There were at least a half dozen fires burning in the upper seats. I felt like one of those cavalry scouts looking into the hills and being surrounding by these campfires. Then somebody said they heard sirens."

What Tingelhoff was seeing was a preventive strike against winter by the Lions' more practical fans. They built those fires in the upper decks to keep warm. Nobody was sure whether they brought in kindling or ripped up some seats. I remember the scene. The fans were festive and probably half-oiled but there's no question they were staying warm. Tingelhoff remembers being envious. "If we had any sense we would have gone up there to join them." They probably would have arrived late. The cops got there ahead of the fire crews and the campfires were out before the stadium went up in flames. I asked one of my pals in the Detroit press, Joe Falls, whether he expected any charges to be filed. "Hell, no," he said. "Those seats are so bad they *should* have been burned."

But neither Forbes nor Tiger Stadium or any of the others touched Wrigley as a forum for all-around zany football events of the kind in which Ferguson, Tarkenton, Van Brocklin and the citizens' irregular band starred that Sunday in 1962. It might have been the presence of George Halas, who was without argument the most important single personality in the creation of professional football in America. Halas was the emperor of Wrigley in the fall and, in its early years, of the National Football League. He founded the Bears and was the ramrod in the founding of the NFL out of the semipro potato patches. Its original owners were a grubbing assembly of roughneck football coach-promoters and businessmen who recognized the country's mounting enthusiasm for college football and decided there was a place for marketing a game played by hired pros. It was the frontier era of pro football. Nobody knew what lay beyond. It was also not very far from the stock market crash. The owners were no dunces. They kept a padlock on the cash registers and a stranglehold on the players' wages, which amounted to a few bucks a game. But that was a modus operandi that Halas held onto until the end of his reign in the 1980s and cheerfully fit in with his nickel-squeezing instincts. They led him, in fact, to the role of the Minnesota Vikings' godfather.

The pioneers in the creation of the Vikings, Max Winter, Bill Boyer and H.P. Skoglund of Minneapolis, looked at the NFL scene in the late 1950s. They found themselves being frozen out of a league franchise by the Scrooge impulses of the NFL owners, who frowned on interlopers' sharing their stash with them. It didn't occur to the NFL owners until the next generation that they could extract huge fees out of the eager initiates by selling franchises at vastly inflated prices. In the late '50s and early '60s, Baron Hilton in Los Angeles, Harry Wismer in New York and Lamar Hunt and Bud Adams in Texas felt the same chill that blew on the first Viking owners. But they commanded more money than the combined cash of the NFL. Their response was to organize the American Football League in Minneapolis in 1959. Winter, Boyer and Skoglund threw in with the new league. In Chicago, warning gongs sounded in the office of George Halas. He wasn't worried about an apprentice football league playing ball in Texas or Los Angeles or New York. He *was* worried about pro football competition just 400 miles away in Minneapolis-St. Paul. Halas made some phone calls to Bert Bell, the NFL commissioner, to Wellington Mara of the Giants, to Art Rooney of the Steelers and a few other of the NFL's warhorses. Not long afterward Winter got a call from Halas.

"The NFL would be proud," Halas said, "to offer Minnesota a franchise. What do you think?"

Winter, Boyer and Skoglund thought this was a lovely prospect. They brought in Bernie Ridder of the St. Paul newspapers to give St. Paul a presence and later a gentle little tobacco shop owner from Duluth, Ole Haugsrud, who had learned about the wiles of the world as a newspaper carrier whose route included a brothel in Superior, Wisconsin. He was a loveable gnome of a guy with a bald head and an inexhaustible bank of memories of his years as a football promoter. His place on the original Viking board was not only a gesture of respect to the frost-covered citizens of Duluth but an obligation the rest of the owners couldn't escape. Ole owned one of the original NFL franchises in the 1920s, the Duluth Eskimos. The Eskimos lasted only a couple of years before getting lost in the fjords of finance. In exchange for the right to dump the Eskimos, the NFL gave Ole the right of first refusal on any new franchise granted in Minnesota, a prerogative personally guaranteed by Halas. On the record at least, Ole thus became the first NFL owner (with 10 percent of the stock) whose credentials included servicing a whorehouse.

It couldn't have happened without Halas. This was the same George Halas who brought Red Grange into pro ball to barnstorm the country and mine some of the cash that had been going exclusively to college football. He was also the same canny capitalist who sold seats on the end of the Bears' player bench. I suppose you could call that tacky. It probably was. You could also call it far-sighted, although not many people who knew Halas called it that. Four decades later the whole National Football League was doing essentially the same thing by building luxury private suites for the fat cats. Most of the suites, of course, were financed with taxpayers' funds. For these, the NFL clubs charged the fat cats massive money to sit in them so that the fat cats could show off their wealth to the peons—whose money subsidized the suites—and show off their power to their clients.

Back in midcentury, George Halas thought the citizens' band was nifty. The citizen musicians, after all, were volunteers, a concept that appealed to George's sense of thrift. In pro football's early years in the 1920s, the wages of the players were so niggardly that the heroes actually made $10 bets on their teams in the middle of the game, grunting the stakes across the line of scrimmage. This is truth. It comes from the joyous testimony of Johnny Blood, the Shakespeare-quoting, college math professor of later years who was one of pro football's incorrigible rogues in his playing years. The players' behavior had improved slightly by 1962 when the Vikings and Bears played the game that shattered the musicians at Wrigley. They were settled in their usual seats in the first two rows behind the end zone. The citizens' band had assembled there for years. Compared with the high-powered halftime bands of the times, the volunteer musicians were bratwurst alongside filet mignon. They played polkas, pep tunes and even a mazurka now and then borrowed from Chicago's Polish neighborhoods.

Once the Vikings-Bears game got going that year, the pace of the touchdowns taxed the irregulars' artistic resources. The teams were scoring in bushels, and it was impossible for the musicians to play and stay abreast of the action simultaneously. It was Tarkenton's air strikes against the Bears' brute running game. Tarkenton's chief accomplice that day was Ferguson, who mortified the Bears' fans with his one great day in the National Football League. Charley was a borderline mediocrity the Vikings scraped from the Cleveland Browns' huge vats of football talent. He was 6 feet 5 inches tall and weighed 235 pounds. His legs accounted for at least three-fourths of his vertical profile. On the dead run he was all legs and hips and would have been impossible to handle by the stubby defensive backs of his time if he'd been able to stay healthy. He didn't, but on this day in Chicago he was sound and an irresistible target for Tarkenton. He had already scored twice on Tarkenton passes and now, with the Bears leading by five points late in the game, Ferguson angled one more time for the Bears' end zone. Tarkenton made two loops behind the line to escape the rushing Bears' dreadnoughts. He threw on the run. As the ball arched toward the corner of the end zone, Ferguson seemed too distant to overtake it. But Charley put those long legs in overdrive and snared the ball in full flight just before his feet hit the chalklines. As he did he looked into the bleachers just in time to see the bandsmen scattering in terror to avoid being trampled.

There was no escape. The clarinet player did see him coming and tried to warn his buddies. There wasn't time. The clarinet player was obliterated with the band in full chorus of the "Colonel Bogey March," somebody said later. The "Colonel Bogey March," you'll remember, was featured in the movie *The Bridge Over the River Kwai*. The band had just come to the part where the whole battalion of British prisoners crosses the bridge. It was at this very point in the score where Ferguson struck. A witness a few rows away said the trombones in the front row were defenseless. Ferguson plowed into them at maximum G's. "The worst part about it," the witness said later, "was that he hit them right in the brass."

The air was rent with the sounds of busted valves, splintered brass and the shrapnel of flying tubas. You could excuse the musicians for what happened next. They were not hired for their bravery. They acted no worse than panic-struck infantrymen hit from ambush. Some of them threw away their trumpets and tubas in their panic to escape.

Through this broken array, Ferguson churned invincibly until he hit an exit ramp that allowed him a gradual runout. Behind him was a virtual carnage. The bandsmen were flattened and demoralized. They needed hymnals more than the score sheets of John Philip Sousa.

The misery of the Bears' band was trifling, though, alongside the sudden asphyxiation of the Vikings in the closing moments of the ball game. Ferguson's third touchdown put the Vikings in the lead, which they promptly lost to a Bears' field goal. But late in the fourth quarter the Vikings' barged back down the field. Doug Mayberry was a rookie Viking fullback with a blacksmith's biceps. He was too rustic to be awed by the Bears' reputation. Late in the drive he hit straight up the middle for 12 yards to the Bears' goal line. The officials put the ball on the 6-inch line. From the sidelines, Van Brocklin screamed and turned purple. "You blind bastards," he yelled, "it's a touchdown. You ought to be jailed. He was in!"

He probably was, but the officials said he wasn't. The ball stayed 6 inches away from the goal. In two more plays it was farther back than that and Jim Christopherson kicked a field goal to restore the Vikings' 2-point lead. The Bears counterattacked and reached the Viking 20 but with 35 seconds left, Billy Butler intercepted a pass and the Bears were dead and buried.

The only way they could be disinterred was by recapturing the ball through an interception or fumble. The Vikings naturally declined to pass. Young Tarkenton, calling the plays, knew the Vikings could run out the clock with one more play.

So he called a handoff to Mayberry.

Simple enough. Isn't that right? You want to remember that in those years, a quarterback putting his knee down to protect the ball wasn't the football dogma that it is today. There are two fundamental reasons it is dogma today. One was the improbable act of the New York Giants' quarterback, Joe Pisarcek, who tried to seal a Giants' victory on the final play by turning with the ball and adroitly extending his arm to hand the ball to his oncoming fullback. The fullback got there just in time to see a lineman from the other side spear the ball from Pisarcek and run for a touchdown that beat the Giants.

The other reason that quarterbacks kneel with the ball today is the legacy of the Minnesota Vikings in Chicago. Francis called Mayberry into the line. Obviously Mayberry was going to surround the football with his black-smith's muscles. That certainly was Tarkenton's intention, to say nothing of Mayberry's. Nobody made Ed O'Bradovich part of the deal. O'Bradovich was a Bears' defensive end who was mean and snarly and 6-feet-6. Remarkably, nobody blocked him on the play. O'Bradovich charged into the Viking backfield and grabbed both Tarkenton and Mayberry as they were exchanging the ball, which wound up on the ground in custody of the Bears.

The officials stopped the clock on the change of possession. Roger LeClerc kicked a field goal for the Bears and the Vikings lost. On the sidelines, Van Brocklin seethed in a dilemma. Should he go after Tarkenton for the dumbest decision in recorded history, or hammer the officials for their call on the goal line? Tarkenton made it an easy choice by disappearing into the Wrigley dungeons before the officials got off the field. So Van Brocklin pursued the officials. He did it apoplectically. His face went grape with rage. He denounced the officials' utter lack of gonads. He hounded them across the field and into the tunnels. He accused them of carrying water for Halas.

He said they were freaks, without brains, eyes or spines. None of them changed speed for fear of missing one defamatory syllable they could put in their official report.

When he got to the locker room, Van Brocklin turned the press conference into a nonstop monologue of profanity. When he finished with the officials, somebody asked about the handoff to Mayberry. That was the end of the line for Van Brocklin. He didn't want to talk about Mayberry or Tarkenton. What he did was to lay the wood to the reporters for asking stupid questions. Having finished with this erudite analysis of the game, the Dutchman kicked the reporters out of his office.

I talked to Tarkenton a few days later.

"Did the Dutchman chew you out in the team meeting for calling that handoff?" I asked.

"It wasn't bad by the Dutchman's standards," Tarkenton replied. "He said it was the kind of chowderhead call you'd expect from a quarterback just out of nursery school."

"So he didn't spend an hour screaming at you for the handoff play."

"No. He spent an hour screaming at the guy who missed the block on O'Bradovich."

"Do you sympathize with that guy?"

"Hell, no. He almost got me killed."

There was a predictable moral in all of this. Tarkenton survived the embarrassing play. The Bears survived the near defeat in the middle of 1962 to become the National Football League champions in 1963.

The lineman who missed the block on O'Bradovich was gone the next season, never to be heard from again.

"The guys who don't know football are the ones who tell you the quarterback who never won the Super Bowl. . . . [is a bum]. One thing you learn in 40 years of coaching is not to listen to idiots."

–Jerry Burns dismissing the complaint against Fran Tarkenton.

The Bad Rap on
Francis the Unloved

In the summer of 1999, the financial pages of newspapers across the country carried a story about the legal miseries of Francis Tarkenton.

His company was fined heavily by the federal government for allegedly trying to inflate the value of his high-tech operations in Georgia with a scheme to make it appear that sales were higher than they were.

The story is mentioned here because if there was much sympathy for Francis' predicament it wasn't revealed in any outpouring of grief in Minnesota, the land where he played most of his professional football.

Nor were there any confetti showers in the sports bistros in Minneapolis and St. Paul years earlier when Francis was elected to the Hall of Fame in his second year of eligibility. There was a similar lack of jubilation in the neon palisades of New York City, where Tarkenton played for five seasons with the Giants.

Even in his flourishing years as a Super Bowl quarterback, Francis Tarkenton fostered little love among the multitudes who watched him break most of professional football's passing records that existed then. Early in his career they did marvel at him. His audacious scampering miles behind the line of scrimmage to salvage a play, the command he exuded—and the numbers he piled up—gave him respect and literally made him unique. The crowds were captivated although the sourdoughs of pro ball looked at him as something of a freak. His ad lib scurrying violated the codes of conduct of the quarterback fraternity, they said. If you played the position right, they said, you planted yourself in the pocket formed by your blockers. If the rush collapsed the pocket, you took the hammering and ate the football or threw it into the 10th row. This logic was pretty much engraved as the creed of the quarterback-gladiator in pro football.

Tarkenton said to hell with falling on your sword. If there was a way to save the play, start running. Buy some time. It would take years before pro football accepted Francis Tarkenton's seat-of-the-pants behavior and called it "mobility," a more dignified word than "scrambling." Tarkenton outgrew his wild freelancing at about the time he found himself in the huddle with quality football teams that could insulate the quarterback from decapitation.

Yet for all of his later success, his Pro Bowl years, his three appearances in the Super Bowl and his MVP award, Tarkenton never inspired any hysterical fan clubs. Maybe, especially after his defeats, he was too glib and tart when the journalists surrounded him in the locker room. Some of that spilled into sarcasm. There were more times when he was mischievous in victory, generous in recounting the play of his teammates and sometimes chivalrous toward the losers. That persona didn't reach the public (or the journalists) with the same impact of his sourness on the bad days. He got a reputation for being selfish, a me-first guy. There was some truth in that, although self-interest is hardly new among professional competitors and it rarely affected Tarkenton's performance on the field. Late in his career when his arm weakened, the critics railed that Tarkenton threw puffballs and rags and rotten apples. Probably. His teams still won. But you don't throw 340 touchdowns by dumping the ball to the fullback for 18 years. There were seasons in New York when he was stronger and younger, and when his deep throws to Homer Jones produced gobs of touchdowns for a team devoid of any other competitive virtues.

The record and the verdict of most of the players and coaches who knew him best was that Francis Asbury Tarkenton was an extraordinary football player, resourceful and tough, a man with a nimble mind and nimble feet, a risk-taker who knew how to win.

You will get a different picture of him from Ron Yary, a powerhouse offensive lineman on the Viking teams of the '70s and '80s, who himself deserves to be in the Hall of Fame. Yary was an introspective guy, sometimes a brooder and a kind of silent judge of the human condition in the huddle. Yary conceded Tarkenton's ability to orchestrate an offense. He didn't care for him personally. To Yary, Tarkenton had to express his individualism all the time, in the way he played and in his breezy, verbal locker-room style. Tarkenton's teams had a tendency, Yary thought, to be just too-much Tarkenton. That judgment was not unanimous among

Viking players of the '60s and '70s. You didn't hear it from Bud Grant or Jerry Burns, the team's offensive coordinator at the time of its biggest seasons in the '70s.

Maybe Tarkenton's problem with football immortality had nothing much to do with popularity. Although he was by far the most visible star on the teams he played for, Tarkenton didn't look very heroic if you compared him with the heroic profiles of quarterbacks like John Unitas, Roger Staubach, Bart Starr, Bob Griese and Kenny Stabler, his contemporaries, and later Joe Montana and Dan Marino. You have to ignore Terry Bradshaw's television slapstick to remember that he, too, belongs in the same elite assembly. On the record, so does Tarkenton. On the field, he winged it and played "Frantic Francis" in his early era. Later he presided over what was the de facto first West Coast offense, distributing the ball to a half dozen receivers from a maze of formations concocted by Burns. He kept ringing up touchdowns but not much affection and any special awe from the galleries because–

He didn't win in the Super Bowl.

Neither did Grant, who followed Tarkenton into the Hall of Fame. But Grant was excused for not winning in the Super Bowl. Among the Viking masses, Grant was truly epochal. He seemed to have emerged as an engraving from the Canadian glaciers and the cliffs of Lake Superior. He was impregnable, standing motionless on the sidelines in his mackinaw and headset in the middle of the snow flurries. To the tailgating thousands at the old Metropolitan Stadium, Grant seemed to belong on Mount Rushmore. He had the face for it, especially when it was turned into the wind on a gusty December Sunday at the Met, and the wind-chill stood at -20. Ballplayers bounced up and down around him, hands jammed into their warm-up jackets, trying to extract some shred of heat from their exertions. Grant just stood there invincibly without moving an eyelash, like some mythological god heedless of the earthly elements. Once in a while his players would look furtively in his direction to see if he saw them slip their fingers into the contraband lumberjack gloves they had hidden in the pockets. Grant banned gloves. He banned butane heaters. Moony Winston, the Viking linebacker, said he wouldn't be surprised if Grant banned helmets.

On the first winter day each year, Grant preached a terse philosophy that became the 11th Commandment of all Viking teams that played outdoors at the old Met: It's going to be cold in December, he said. *You're* going to be cold. Accept that and play in it. The other guys are going to hate it. They're going to spend all their time on the field thinking about the heater on the sideline. When they do that, it takes their minds off football and they spend most of the game thinking how miserable they are. That's advantage to us. So use it.

The Viking players rarely broke into boisterous applause when they heard that speech. They did live with it and secretly congratulated themselves on being able to play like human polar bears. They knew what was going on in the minds of the miserable Rams, thronged around their heaters a few yards away, freshly arrived from the Pacific beaches. "These guys [the Vikings] are from Mars," the Rams would be telling themselves. "How are we going to beat them playing on ice?"

They never did.

So the Viking crowds saw Grant as some sort of man of ice out of the North, if not something heroic then least something immovable and time-less, a part of their environment. His homey axioms titillated them: "Sometimes you win just by showing up." But when somebody asked him why the Vikings kept losing in the Super Bowl, they never quite bought Grant's solemn explanation, for all of their admiration for him. Their own explanations sounded a lot more plausible: The Vikings didn't play with enough emotion. They weren't ready for warm weather football. Tarkenton was the bummer.

Grant told them: "When you get rid of all that speculation, which is pretty much garbage, you have to figure that usually when you lose it's because the other guys are better." Which meant that the Vikings' audiences were being told to consider the unthinkable: that the Viking teams of (first) Joe Kapp, and then Tarkenton, of Carl Eller, Alan Page, Jim Marshall, Mick Tingelhoff, Ron Yary, Paul Krause and Bill Brown were not as good as the four teams that zonked them in the Super Bowl. You might remember the teams that beat the Vikings in the Super Bowl. They were hardly ham-burger ball clubs, beginning with the Kansas City Chiefs of Lennie Dawson, Bobby Bell. Willie Lanier and Buck Buchanan. They were followed by the Miami Dolphins of Griese, Larry Csonka, Jim Langer, Paul Warfield and Larry Little, the Pittsburgh Steelers of Bradshaw, Mean Joe Greene, Jack Ham and Franco Harris, and finally the Raiders of Stabler, Gene Upshaw, Fred Biletnikoff and Jack Tatum.

Each time you look at those rosters you come a little closer to Grant's prag-matic theory about why the Vikings lost. But when Grant talked like that, the Viking fans mentally told Grant to go feed his dogs. The idea, they said, was preposterous. No way were those teams better than the Vikings. Grant, they said, was entitled to his quirks; and he probably was trying to protect Tarkenton.

Tarkenton, after all, was on the field for all but one of those embarrassments. He took the fall. If that was his destiny, it didn't wreck his enjoyment of being Francis Tarkenton. He played reasonably well in all of those games. Football was the largest piece of his life from July to January, but increasingly he was a juggler of his steadily whirling agendas: football, a motivation business, a television show in New York, speeches, family, investments, books, the industry of being Francis Tarkenton. A few of his teammates resented that, but one of them, Alan Page, viewed Tarkenton's breathless capitalizations less with envy than with anger. Alan Page was a defensive lineman with the Vikings. He had been its best player for several years before Tarkenton returned to the Vikings in 1972 after his five years with the Giants. Tarkenton was flooded with endorsement offers the day of his second coming to the cornfields. Alan Page had been named the league's most valuable player a year before, the first NFL lineman so honored. He drew a blank in endorsements. Tarkenton was white, Page was black. Page exhibited no personal animosity toward Tarkenton. He did wonder about society and its values, and particularly the advertising agencies and their values.

The fans' disaffection with Tarkenton was never very harsh. Tarkenton did go public a few times when the jeers he heard late in his career punctured his generally sophisticated skin. They booed him in a few games when the offense stagnated and they wanted to see more of the new fireball from Texas, Tommy Kramer. Tarkenton's notions of decorum were stung. "Hey," he said, "in most places they revere players who've been through the battles. I think those players are entitled to that."

The word "revere" may not be the precise one Francis was aiming for. He might have meant something closer to dignity and respect. Revere is probably not what the spectators are going to do with a patriarchal quarterback who has just thrown an interception. But the judgments he heard from his peers or from the media booths never provoked any crisis in Tarkenton's professional life. He was satisfied with his performance. He was satisfied with Francis Tarkenton in general. He knew more about football than his critics, he knew when an interception was his blunder and when it was the fault of a receiver who made the wrong cut, or simply when it resulted from an exceptional play by a defensive back. He didn't think he had to explain the distinctions.

But there was a streak of the psychologist in him. Tarkenton loved to probe the reasons why, particularly as they affected the game he played. Why did this player behave like a cabbage head when the crunch was in and why did that one dig into his guts to stop a play on the goal line–and never ask for credit? What impelled the fans to hurl their profanity on a player who missed a catch, a man who shouldn't have been playing in the first place because he was playing half dead from exhaustion. The psychology of the game intrigued him. He kept bouncing his theories off the defenseless head of Mick Tingelhoff, his roommate, and the even more vulnerable heads of the writers covering the team. He had theories that tried to link ethnic background to the positions the athletes played. Linebackers, he said, often came with southern and middle European genes because linebacking was all about passion and encounter and he gave you the names of Dick Butkus, Ray Nitschke and Bill George. African-Americans tended to be swift, tended to be leapers and highly athletic, and they were the receivers and defensive backs. And quarterbacks? Well, there were a lot of south-erners playing quarterback then in the NFL. Tarkenton would noodle about this and find different explanations but he would doubt that it was coincidence. Today, of course, his theories are shot full of holes because there are African-Americans prospering in all the positions and the world's ethnics are scattered all over the football field at all positions. But Tarkenton would then be off on a psychoanalysis of the crowds. People lived crammed together and on top of each other in the big urban centers, he said, which is why you could expect the worst rowdyism from crowds in New York, Philadelphia and Chicago. Their behavior at a ball game reflected their social hostilities. Stadiums in the midlands, he theorized, in Kansas City, Green Bay and in the Twin Cities, were slightly more civilized.

Since I happen to live in the Twin Cities, I have to note that it was at Metropolitan Stadium where a fan threw a whisky bottle that creased the head of an official named Armen Terzian. He was the official who ruled it a completed pass from Staubach to Drew Pearson in the last minute of a playoff game, the celebrated Hail Mary play. The Vikings lost, and it has to be further noted that the bottle flew out of the stands at about the moment Tarkenton's tirade against Terzian incited the crowd.

But why should that tilt Francis Tarkenton? He spread his roles around–quarterback, philosopher, and provocateur. Boredom was banned from the Tarkenton agenda. And after the first few years of pro ball, he rarely expected to be surprised by what he heard and saw from the viewing public. Loyalty usually lasted until the next interception. It is the way of professional ball, he decided early. Live with it. Don't be poisoned by it.

Re-enter the psychologist. "Where does the fan get this deep emotional involvement in this game that can turn him into an absolute maniac?" Francis once asked me. Tarkenton's mind jumps around mercurially. When we talked his rhetorical questions usually allowed scant time for answers and weren't intended to. When he got no immediate profundity from me, he provided his own. "I think his involvement with football momentarily removes some of the confusion from the fan's life. There's disunity in his world. He's not sure he's making progress or not. In football, it's win or lose. Every game is like that, baseball, hockey, the rest, but pro football is mass-produced on TV. It's in everybody's life. Fans can be very perceptive but when they're in the stadium or in front of the TV screen, they want life to be simple. When they're watching football, the gray areas of life are out of the picture. They want a result, when the images they have of their players are either confirmed or repudiated. It must be hell to be a hockey fan and go home with the score 3-3.

"I've been exposed to every kind of reaction from the fans from acclaim to demands for my head. Thrown in with 60,000 others, the fan may sound tremendously appreciative and loyal, or tremendously insane. I remind myself of that all the time. Away from the game these people may be entirely different personalities. I think that many of them when they're in the stadium are privately gratified over the distress or defeat of a famous athlete. I think it pleases this kind of fan to know that even famous or moneyed athletic heroes have to bow to the humiliations of life. Maybe the fan isn't aware of it, but I've been in too many stadiums and heard too many crowds to question it.

"Should that make me bitter? Not at all. We all fill roles for each other, one way or another."

That is a civil attitude to take.

But Tarkenton did feel bitter some days, about fans, about being judged as one of the quarterbacks who never won the Super Bowl. Because he liked to be seen as a worldly guy, not often fazed by the opinions of the hoi polloi or ignoramuses in the press box, he usually laughed off the slams. When he confronted them, he usually got tangled up in rhetoric. There was the "revere" business. When somebody asked him what quarterbacks needed to be successful, his menu included "arrogance." This probably makes sense to quarterbacks. It didn't have much box office appeal with the Minnesota public.

I met him on his first day in training camp of July in 1961. I liked him then. I still remember him fondly and with respect as a ballplayer. About his business m.o., I don't know much. Whatever corporate muddles he got into were predictable. From the beginning, he was fascinated by what went on in the mahogany offices and the whole corporate whirl. It captivated him in the way sailing the ocean might captivate the weekend sailor on Lake Harriet. There was something big and available out there if you engaged it head-on with your brains and energy and reasonable amounts of gall. He was a communicator. He could do that instinctively in the huddle and in front of the TV cameras. That might have been part of the problems that reached the government in his later years. He learned to talk the talk well before learning the walk.

But I don't really judge him that way.

As a ballplayer, Tarkenton understood that the high-profile athlete's role in the life of the fan is more than being a performer. Football fans sooner or later, intensely or casually, link their identities with the player's, and if the athlete doesn't recognize that, he played his amateur ball in a monastery. For millions of football fans, it's more than entertainment that they want. The battle and the goal become personal. When the Viking kickoff team makes its banzai charge downfield, it's all glands and exposed teeth, bent on destroying and burying the return man. The special teams on kickoffs are acting out the basic law of the jungle. But all of that frothing passion is not confined to the ballplayers. The fan sees and feels it. He's roaring down the field with the kickoff team, transported into the swirl of flying bodies and general mayhem from his arena seat or from his television. It's happening in Warroad and it's happening in Winona. Don't tell these people it's just a game. For the vacationing visitor from Trondheim, Norway, innocently trapped in his relatives' living room on a Sunday afternoon in Bloomington, the shrieks and clenched fists have to look comical. Nobody could be that maniacal about a football game.

But we know better, don't we? The ballplayer should know better. For three hours, he is going to be the alter ego of all those shrieking people. Which means the egos are joined. The fan might just as well be wearing a helmet and birdcage when he chews on his chicken leg in front of the screen. He is inseparable from his team. And when the team fails, it is not simply defeat.

It is betrayal. When it happens two weeks in a row it is unbelievable. When it happens three weeks in a row, it is unforgivable.

It took Tarkenton a year or two to figure that out, but he had the tough crust of the uncompromising competitor and he was never much intimidated by the harpoons of the crowd or of resentful ballplayers. Most of the people who played with him appreciated that competitiveness and the quick mind that went with it. The players were a lot more stable in their judgments than the fan with his sudden shifts of love to loathing, depending on what happened on third down.

Paul Flatley, the flanker with the Vikings in the mid-1960s, found something to admire both in Tarkenton and Van Brocklin, whose antagonism toward Tarkenton deepened with their years together. Tarkenton was Flatley's benefactor with his improvised passes that usually managed to locate Paul Flatley after all of the chaos Tarkenton wrought behind the line of scrimmage.

"The way Tarkenton impressed the ballplayer who huddled with him," Flatley said, "was that he was a take-charge guy who took advantage of everything anybody gave him on the field. There were a few people on the team who felt that sometimes he was more concerned with himself than he was about anything else. I never paid that much attention. You hear that about any successful person. And Tarkenton had a great desire to be successful personally. It wasn't confined to the football field, of course. He was one of the first guys in pro ball who was seriously planning a business career and working at it while he was still playing. I don't know many guys who had trouble getting along with him. He was a talkative, breezy guy in the locker room. Away from there, he was more aloof from the guys than most ballplayers are, even the stars.

"Part of that was because he didn't have much of a role at our beer parties at that stage of his career, and part of it might have been that he just didn't care much for mob scenes.

"He scrambled around the field in his early years, sure. But the players weren't going to criticize that. They knew the problems of an expansion team trying to win in those years, and they also knew that Tarkenton had abilities that were unique in a quarterback. Not anybody who played quarterback for the Vikings could have motored around that way with any chance of reaching old age. Tarkenton and I never worked on any cues or plans to use when the play went into one of those playground routines. Everything was strictly on the fly. You see versions of that now and then in today's football, especially from Brett Favre and Doug Flutie. But with Tarkenton it was a real gas, a one-man jail break. He actually looped around so horrendously one day in Los Angeles that he found himself 45 yards behind the line of scrimmage and I think Cliff Livingston tackled him there, which pretty well shot the hell out of our rushing yardage for the game. He did it 8 or 10 times a game. The only rule was that you tried to get on the same side of the field where Tarkenton was headed. You hear the announcers pounding away on that idea today. But Tarkenton and I practically invented it, because until then there wasn't anybody in pro ball who did it as often as Tarkenton and so recklessly and yet with a pretty good idea of where he was and where the potential disaster was coming from. I want to tell you it wasn't always easy to tell where he was headed, because he headed for different sides of the field on some of those plays. All I did was try to pick out a spot he could see and then run that way waving my arms. I wasn't very fast or very big or any kind of Hall of Famer. But I had about as much gall as he did, and you'd be surprised how many passes I caught doing that."

The retrospectives on Tarkenton as a quarterback usually elevate him to the level of a prodigy because he was a starter from his rookie season and clearly understood the game with uncommon perception. He reflected the confidence of a man who had it pretty well figured out by his second or third season. Tarkenton knows the pro game better than to have ever made such claims. Years after he finished his career, his old sparring partner at the Viking bargaining tables, Mike Lynn, supplied some testimony to Tarkenton's candor on that point. "He told me often," Lynn said, "that it took him at least five years to read the defenses the way a veteran quarterback needs to, and he said he didn't know many or any quarterbacks who wouldn't tell you the same thing."

But he was the boss in the huddle, all right.

Flatley again: "I can't remember anyone confronting him. Every now and then somebody would do some yipping about this or that in the huddle, and Tarkenton would say, 'hey, goddammit,' and that was the end of it."

To be credible about Tarkenton's tenure with the Vikings, I need to note that I wrote a book with him in the mid-1970s. Despite the lacings he took from part of the media clan in the '70s and thereafter, his relations were comfortable with most of the people who covered him locally and, for that matter, most of the media generally. He lapped up all of the Super Bowl's pregame banter that is now part of the much-reviled "media hype." He was good at it, and he initiated much of the repartee. In fact, on the team bus from the hotel to the stadium for road games, you couldn't shut him up in his later years. He needled people like Lynn and Sid Hartman, the omnipresent sports columnist in Minneapolis. He did it ruthlessly and profanely. He would pretend to be a sportscaster and roast all pomposities available in the bus, real and invented. Lynn loved those virtual reality brawls and was the last guy on earth to be handicapped by charity or good taste when it came to Tarkenton's pomposities. It might have been a way for Tarkenton to valve off some of his pregame adrenaline surges. But it probably wasn't. Playing football, living in the football environment, kept him revved up from start to finish in his 18 years in the game.

This was the preacher's kid swiftly transformed from the choir boy mentality he brought into pro football (no booze, no chasing, no dockwalloper language) to the worldly, crusty old pro of his celebrity seasons. He came into it as a third-round draft choice with a starting salary of $12,000 in 1961. He left it making $400,000–which was major cash in the 1970s. He threw four touchdown passes in his first game in the National Football League, to the bilious astonishment of George Halas of the Bears, who created the league. He left with so little regard for the required postures of the departing star that in his last game in football–knowing he was going to retire in a few months–he refused to make any heroic statements on the field. He could have done that by throwing for the end zone on his last series of a game against the Rams, already decided. Ted Williams hit a home run in his last game. Francis Tarkenton ran the ball into the line three times and, grinning, walked off the field. Hardly a gesture of love and sentiment.

Still, I respected him without overlooking his personal or corporate opportunism. He shed most of his football pals quickly once he retired, an act that probably reflected less on his lack of personal loyalty than it did his impatience to soar into the waiting galaxies of his new corporate worlds. Not all of football's departing jocks hang onto the roughhouse camaraderie of the locker room as religiously as some do. What I liked most about Tarkenton as a ballplayer was his core toughness. He concealed his injuries and played through them with the same hammerhead attitude as the hairiest linebackers.

Bud Grant knew that. He also knew something about Tarkenton's nature and his instincts for the rough bonding that has to go on with a ball club.

Tarkenton also knew that the bonding is always better when it doesn't have to be orchestrated with speeches or slogans. There *were people* on the team that didn't care for him. "But when you watched him at one of our practices," Grant said, "it was a tip-off to the environment he liked to play in. I'd be willing to bet a small steak that sooner or later he had a word with everybody on the field, every player, coach, ball boy and water sprinkler. I never saw him as a politician. What he looked like to me was a fellow who fills out his life with something meaningful whatever he's doing. You had to tell yourself, 'here's a guy who involves himself.' He might have walked by a rookie receiver and offer a suggestion about how the rookie could improve one of his pass patterns. He'd walk by Carl Eller and razz him about his new hat. He'd mimic Jerry Burns a little. More than a little. He was always interacting. Those instincts extended to how he played the game. Nobody figured out how he was able to survive all those years when he was charging around behind the line. He got away with it because he had a sense for it. He knew when to turn or throw or run because he sensed the pressure or the open man.

"What the coach admires in a ballplayer are not only his skills and toughness but his maturity. He'd learned how to accept the outcome of the game, which kept him in balance as an athlete. Some guys after a big win will walk around starry-eyed for days or look like they heard bad news from the bank when they lost. Tarkenton had it as well organized as any athlete I've seen, and for that reason you knew that when he went out on the field on Sunday, nobody could possibly be more ready to direct a football team."

So, all right. If the guy brought that much to the field, threw all of those touchdown passes, set records, pioneered the quick-release, ball-distribution offense with Jerry Burns—the one we now call West Coast—why isn't he on that roster of Super Bowl winners?

"Why in the hell would you ask me?" Jerry Burns huffed. "All I did was coach football for 40 years. Don't ask me to give you the answers about football. A lot of guys in the Hall of Fame, and a lot more who deserve to be, never won the Super Bowl. All I know about Tarkenton from coaching him was this: You'll get quarterbacks with their team on the other guy's 6-yard line. Third down. They call it the red zone today. When I coached they called it the 6-yard line. And you're talking to the quarterback on the sideline and you can tell he's worried about taking heat if you don't get into the end zone. So he'll say something like, 'I think that trap play will go here.' Or maybe a draw. What he's saying is 'Coach, I'm not sure I want to throw it.' With Tarkenton what you got was 'Burnsie, give me a rollout, something where they have to guess and I've got more time to throw. We're gonna get in there. Damned if we're not.' What he was saying was 'let me do it.' He was going to throw or run but what he really was going to do was throw it into the end zone and he could care less about taking heat if he didn't get in there. Those are the guys you want on third and six."

You didn't have to love such a man to know that he was a player. The roster of Minnesota Viking alumni who got to Super Bowl but never won is impressive. It includes Bud Grant, Alan Page, Paul Krause and Francis Tarkenton. All of them are now in the game's Hall of Fame. No special stigma attaches to coaches, defensive linemen and defensive backs who made the Hall of Fame but didn't win the Super Bowl. Quarterbacks are different. If they didn't win it, they are privately consigned by their critics to the outhouse of Hall of Fame quarterbacks.

Burns' judgment about that is bald and blunt. "The guys who really know football don't give a damn about which quarterback won the Super Bowl. The guys who don't know football are the ones who tell you the quarterback who never won the Super Bowl doesn't belong with the others. One thing you learn in 40 years of coaching is not to listen to idiots."

So he didn't and doesn't. When you talk quarterbacks to Burns, you might want to put Francis Tarkenton near the head of the conversation. If you don't, the conversation is probably going to end in a hurry.

"What those guys are saying with all that stuff [showoff mugging for the camera and self-congratulations after a play] is 'me. I did it.' Throw that out. It doesn't belong in football."

—ESPN broadcaster

The Idiot Mating Dances in the End Zone

*I*n the middle of the 1999 football season, the millionaire Huckleberry Finn of the pro game and probably its No. 1 matinee hero, Green Bay's Brett Favre, charged downfield in a game against the Detroit Lions. He got into the face of a Lions' defensive back and made a triumphant slashing gesture across his own throat.

The Packers had just hit it big on the field. Favre's face was lit by a rush of personal vengeance. It translated: "I'm slitting your throats, Lions. You did it to me the last time we played."

It was a spontaneous act of malice that combined with Favre's familiar spasms of exuberance and nuttiness. Millions saw it on television. They not only saw it live, they saw it recycled every day for the next seven days. You saw it live Sunday afternoon, warmed over Sunday night, Monday morning, Monday afternoon and a dozen more times from 3 a.m. to midnight if you needed that much football on television, which mobs of people clearly do, In fact, even normal people saw it a dozen times during the ensuing week. Pro football has become that kind of narcotic in American television.

The glut of reruns wasn't confined to Favre. Within hours, the cables were showing every prior act of throat-cutting pantomimed in the heat of action in the NFL in 1999. It was the old gloating revenge act carried to its newest level of vaudeville. In New York, the godfathers of the NFL establishment weren't amused. They shouldn't have been. As pro football's newest hotdog act, the throat-cutting schtick seemed a more offensive version of the old taunting burlesques, where the trash-talking victor would wag his tongue at the sprawled safety. If he didn't do that, he tried plant the football down the safety's throat by spiking it in the end zone. It was all intended to deepen the humiliation of the safety and to let the guy who scored tell the world "he's a piece of crap and I'm the greatest who ever lived."

In his living room, the dormant old newshawk sifted through all of this hash of self-indulgent strutting and mugging. And he groaned. Didn't anybody just line up and hit the guy across the line anymore? And get up and do it again? No, he didn't because he was a fat, 350-pound nose tackle and he only played one down each series. It was one more picture of football of the changing millennia: broad asses hauling down $2 million to fill up space on the line of scrimmage. For a moment I sympathized with the nose tackle, who had to be suffering from job insecurity. In two years he was going to rendered obsolete by a 400-pound nose tackle.

Right about there in my living room, I wanted to pause for an attitude check. It seemed like the only honorable thing to do. But I found myself distracted for the 75th time by the commercial featuring a klutzy referee who couldn't find a coin to toss and was reduced to asking the players to cash a dollar bill so he could start the game.

At this impasse on the screen, I found myself laughing. God, how many times were they going to play it? I'd sifted through all this slapstick scene-stealing by the pros of today, and I remembered a rookie receiver named Sammy White of the Vikings in the mid-1970s. Sammy was a likeable kid who thought he would get into the flow of the celebration stunts that were sweeping the league. It was the first attempt at let-it-hang-out showmanship in the regime of Harry Peter Grant, the head coach. There were three things I remembered about it particularly. A. Sammy's stunt was a fiasco. B. The Viking coach decided not to be appalled. What he decided to be was paternal. He gave Sammy a brief sideline lecture. Being Harry P. Grant, he lectured briefly and as privately as he could in front of 50,000 people. He didn't do it with any special warmth. Harry P. Grant did almost nothing warmly except to pet his dog. He did make an impression. According to all statisticians, nobody in Grant's employment by the Vikings ever repeated Sammy's act.

And C. Sammy's mom blistered him by telephone not long afterward, about which more a little later.

In some ways the throat-cutting epidemic of 1999 broke new ground in the increasing urge by some of today's pro football players to gross out on camera. One result, abhorrent to the NFL administrators, was to put the National Football League one step closer to the sideshows of professional wrestling. Recognizing this, the NFL administrators squirmed and promised retribution in the form of bigger fines.

There are times when the NFL makes itself absurdly pompous. This wasn't one of them. Of all the faces that pro football has put to its public as the unchallenged show of shows in American athletics, the most unsightly one to masses of its watchers is the grotesque exhibitionism they see every Sunday.

Score is 35-10. Tiger Sharks are losing, their fifth in a row. The game is two minutes from over and a Tiger Shark tackle throws the running back for a 2-yard loss. Tiger Shark tackle explodes out of the mess and races 20 yards to the middle of the field. He pounds his chest. He points to his number. Me. I'm the guy. I did it. Remember that number. We're losing by a ton but I just made the play of the year and I don't want anybody else taking credit. I could be headed for Canton with that play.

Television camera dutifully records all of this profound drama, granting the Tiger Shark tackle a forum to parade his heroism.

On the Tiger Shark bench, the coach closes his eyes in disgust and dies a little. If you've followed pro football with any kind of awareness over the years, you know this scene is absurd and a cartoon. You also know that you're probably going to get the same scene when the winners play defense in the last minute. A guy sacks the Tiger Shark quarterback. His team is leading 35-10 and he bolts away from his teammates' feeble attempts to get some camera time of their own by hugging him. He does more than run away from them so No. 1 can hog the camera. He *bulls* his way through them. He actually rampages through them, and now the whole world knows who made the sack and probably belongs in Canton.

That is a fair approximation of what happens 20 or 30 times a game in today's pro football. Does that make it a serious eyesore on the fan's enjoyment of the quality of today's football show, as competition and as entertainment?

Maybe not serious. Irritating and tiresome? At least that. Is it bad enough to drive away borderline football watchers on TV, the people who were turned off by the gratuitous barbarism that often infects professional hockey? It might alienate some of them here and there. But that's not what especially worries the NFL impresarios about the idiotic celebratory dances in the end zone (some of which are actually choreographed) and the up-yours taunting that have become pretty standard behavior on Sunday afternoon. What bothers them is the image they project. The NFL is religiously proud of its status as No. 1 in American professional sports, the best show on television. The NFL sees its product as powerfully competitive, filled with appealing personalities and constantly entertaining. In other words, irresistible. The other word it wants in there is "integrity." Still, despite all of its grand visions of Sunday afternoon on American television, it doesn't want to sound stiff and preachy. So it's careful about going too far in cleansing the buffoonery out of the ball game. After all, immature millionaire jerks ought to be allowed to be immature millionaire jerks. So it's not going to tell the Tiger Shark showoff not to act like a fool, which, of course, he is doing. It's not going to do that because every acidic sports columnist in the country is going to rip the NFL with 1,000 words of ridicule and accuse the league of turning its ball fields into kindergartens.

For the same reason it's not going to tell Jamal Anderson of Atlanta that he can't do his Dirty Bird dance after his touchdowns, or Green Bay's Antonio Freeman that he can't trampoline into the adoring end zone crowd at Lambeau Field. To hear the Packer claques tell us, that has become as much of Packer tradition as Vince Lombardi's camel's hair coat. And to be fair about, both of these acts are less than millionaires showing off. They're boys being boys. So they'll keep doing it until somebody gets a hernia. He will if he does the Lambeau Leap once too often and undershoots the end zone wall.

But there ought to be a limit, shouldn't there? That throat-slitting stunt went over the limit in the eyes of the NFL suits in New York because it was too close to the bone. It evoked a violent act. Somebody on the weeknight panel shows put a face on it, remembering a woman named Nicole who got her throat cut, presumably by a former football player. A long reach, that. But it did make this latest contagion look and feel all the more repugnant. Obviously not everybody looked on it that way. Some of the cool clans in the media derided the NFL reaction as childish. This is new generation football, they said. These are players who grew up being prodded by their moms and high school teachers to express themselves. Be open with the world. What's so dirty and malicious about celebrating a touchdown? If the crocks deify the old tradition–Jim Brown runs 70 yards, buries four tacklers and then hands the ball to the official with great dignity–well, let them watch grainy reruns from the 1950s. Let them wear high-top shoes to feel comfortable while they're doing it.

You can make allowances for that argument. This is not the 1950s, for better and for worse. Today we hug everybody in sight from church to the casino. We didn't do that 30 and 40 years ago. People wear T-shirts sprawled with four-letter words in three colors. They didn't 30 years ago. No dialogue in the movies can proceed without three s-words, four f-words and two bs-words in the same paragraph. Gregory Peck and Joan Fontaine didn't talk that way. So the world is different. We act and talk differently. It follows that we play differently and what wasn't allowed or wasn't done 40 years ago is not going to shape how we work and play in a new millennium.

Favre drew 15 yards for unsportsmanlike conduct in the incident last year but was unrepentant in the days afterward. "If I would have been fined I would have been angry," he said. "It's been going on so long, and I do it and it's a topic of discussion all over America. I was just paying the guy back [for happened to Favre in a previous game]."

But Favre and the other throat-cutters got zero tolerance from the resurrected old pros who man the broadcast studios. Sterling Sharpe sounded outraged. So did Tom Jackson and Marty Schottenheimer, joined by their show's mediator, Mike Tirico. "What those guys are saying with all that stuff is 'me. I did it.' Throw that out. It doesn't belong in football."

Ironically, Favre, a high-megaton white football player, might actually have done the cause for racial understanding (and the NFL) a favor by barging in to join the cutthroats. We're dealing now with a subliminal thing, but I think it matters. They don't conduct polls to test the racial attitudes of football publics. But on the issue of exhibitionism in a football game: Most American football watchers probably identify it with the African-American players as guys most likely to be demonstrative, the guys spiking footballs and pounding their chest. Is that stereotype valid? You can go anywhere you want with stereotypes. But the one and probably only one that is valid about showboat football players in the NFL is that most of them are likely to be African-American for one unassailable reason. On any given football field on Sunday, 65 percent of the players will *be* African-Americans.

It may be a valuable footnote to that business to recall that one of the pioneers in the art of hot-dogging after a play was Mark Gastineau, the New York Jets' defensive end who did a war dance over the fallen quarterback after each one of his sacks. And Gastineau was no African-American. Neither is Tim Dwight, the Atlanta receiver and runback man who takes the football and pretends it's a bottle and chugalugs in celebration. It's as obnoxious as the Dirty Bird.

All of this goes to the issue of asserting some reasonable control over the stage mugging, the dizzy spiking of footballs and the ungainly ballets that seem so to fascinate the TV producers. Should it be tempered, banned, what? Well, it's not all going to be banned because there is actually some money involved. Not all of that stuff is purely impulsive. Most of those people know the value of television exposure. One shot of national TV coverage, with millions of eyes on you, and nobody in the camera frame to share the glory with you, makes you more marketable. Or it can. And if you're more marketable the sound bites aren't far behind and if you do enough of it, the endorsements and big-time cameo shots will follow, and the group-song video, and now you're famous, or notorious. Whatever they call it, you're in the big time.

A guy with whom I sometimes watch football groused about the hot-dogging the whole game and finally exploded. "Why in the hell do the cameras keep focusing on these guys?" When you think about it, what else is there to shoot at that moment when the guy is running around pounding his chest. Normally in football, there's a half minute between plays. TV needs constant action, which is why it cranks out four reprises of the previous play. It not only needs continuing action; it lusts after continuing action. Consider what happens when a coach or the officials' booth invokes instant replay. A couple of minutes are going to transpire before the referee emerges from that curtained little cloister where he examines the play from all available angles. For television producers two minutes are eternity. No way is television going to show the backside of that referee with his invisible head in the confessional for two minutes. You are going to get replay, friend. You're going to see it on the screen before the referee renders a decision. You're going to see it not once, twice or three times. You're going to see replays until the referee walks back onto the field, and while you're watching those replays John Madden or Phil Simms is going to be telling you "no question, it was a catch," and then "wait a minute, I don't know if this guy considers that's conclusive proof, or what." So suddenly we have suspense, and TV is in hog heaven awaiting the outcome.

And this is the big reason you see the "look-at-me, I'm-so-great," sideshows by the guy who just made a tackle. A strutting ballplayer showing off in the middle of the field is live action for television. For the producer, the only option between plays is a replay of the tackle the showoff just made. So you get that next. And after that, when the camera comes back live on the field, guess what's happening?

The strutting tackle is still strutting.

If his team is lucky, he gets back onside before the guys on the other side run the next play.

I haven't talked to Sammy White for years and I have no idea to how Sammy views trash talk and the sideshows today. I can't remember Sammy ever talking much trash. He was a little guy from Grambling College, a fellow with a happy soul and restless feet. He was a young man of religious upbringing who tried to respect his elders. He also caught a lot of forward passes from Francis Tarkenton, played in a Super Bowl and almost always behaved in a way that would, in the teachings of his mother, "bring credit to yourself and the family."

But there was a Sunday at Metropolitan Stadium in November of 1976, the year in which Sammy ultimately became the NFL's Rookie of the Year. Sammy was having a big day against the Lions' cornerback, Levi Johnson. If you want to know the truth, Sammy was on fire. He was in the zone, playing out of his mind, catching every ball in sight and running up the numbers. Late in the game, he gave the slip to Levi, broke free and looked for the ball over his shoulder. It arrived on schedule. Sammy caught it and sprinted for the end zone. It was three strides away. He was going in. Sammy never heard any preachment from his mom about not holding the ball over his head in jubilation with the end zone in sight. No way was he going to spike the ball. Coach said he wanted no player of his to do that. But nothing was ever said about holding the ball over his head because he felt so good about playing football and scoring in the NFL. So as he was bounding toward the goal line, Sammy reached up to display his trophy to an admiring world. "I felt so good," he said later, "I wanted to dance and sing. We were ahead and I knew I was about to score the clinching touchdown. And about then I felt this tug on my shoe from somebody's hand [Lem Barney's] and there I went. And there went the ball into the end zone. I saw a guy fall on it [Levi Johnson], and it was the wrong uniform, and I never felt so terrible and miserable."

His route back to the Viking bench steered Sammy unavoidably within the view of Harry P. Grant. It was one of the longest and saddest miles in the anthologies of human remorse. Sammy tried to sort out the possible consequences. Those, he thought, started with suspension and ran through the waiver wire and on to deportation. Instead, Grant spoke briefly. "There's a difference between show biz and showboat," he said. "What you did was showboat. It cost us a touchdown. A player can be happy and show it. But don't be happy by doing something stupid. You'll get another chance."

Grant is not a Hall of Fame football coach for nothing.

A few minutes later the Vikings reached the Detroit 37. Tarkenton called a pass play. Sammy was one of the go-to receivers on the play. Sammy squirmed in his stance across the line of scrimmage from Levi Johnson. Less than two minutes were on the scoreboard. The Vikings' lead was precarious. Sammy talked to himself, and possibly to God. Lord, what had he done? Making a fool of himself, dropping the ball like that. "Please throw me the ball, Francis," he said. "Just one more time."

He glanced down the line at the quarterback chanting his cadence. If anybody could bail him out of his humiliation, Francis Tarkenton could. Francis was his patron, his counselor and his mentor. Mick Tingelhoff snapped the ball. The Lions blitzed their linebackers again. Sammy felt a bolt of hope. It meant that one more time he would race man-on-man against Levi. He gave the cornerback a shoulder and hip and sprinted diagonally across the field. Tarkenton's bodyguards from the offensive line held off the Lion blitzers. Francis lofted the ball deep. It was coming down to him, and Sammy felt the surge of atonement. He grabbed the ball and loped into the end zone to win the game for the Vikings and to run his pass-catching for the day to a Viking record of 210 yards.

He did not hold the ball over his head going into the end zone.

He did not throw the ball into the frozen grass. He did not do a hula in the end zone.

When the officials came for the ball, they were almost forced to pry it away. When he got to the sidelines, Francis Tarkenton hugged him, and he was speechless to think he and the great veteran quarterback were teammates and partners in an important game that thrust the Vikings toward the Super Bowl. After the game, he called home. His mother, having seen it on TV, asked, "Son, did you learn anything today?"

He was explaining what he had learned when his father asked, "Son, do you mind telling your father what in hell you were doing with the ball over your head?"

Naturally, all was forgiven.

I loved little Sammy. I have normal stores of forgiveness. So I can forgive the crazy chest pounding in midfield by the self-indulgent camera hog who just made a meaningless tackle.

I can forgive it but I don't want to watch it. It's an abomination and it belongs in the geek shows.

"We won't see another like him in our lifetimes."

—*Bud Grant, describing Jim Marshall's commitment to his game and his durability.*

Football's
Man of the Ages

Jim Marshall might have been the guy the homesteaders had in mind when they started kicking pumpkins around and called the game football.

We don't know football began that way. It could have been a spinoff from rugby. It could just as easily have been inspired by the great Rendezvous of 1832 out West, when rowdy fur traders clouted and banged into each other for hours in a game patterned after a buffalo stampede. You can still see vestiges of that game on kickoffs in the NFL.

Wilder claims have been made to identify the origins of football. None of them are verifiable. But if they ever mint a coin with the face of the man who personifies the game the inventors intended, you will be looking at the face of Jim Marshall.

Of all of the football players I've known, this is the best fit. The nominations are closed. It should be somebody who would devour the game of football in his exuberance to play it. He would so embody its demands for commitment with all juices flowing every moment on the field, and do it for 283 straight games spread over 19 years, that eventually it could be said (and was): "We won't see another like him in our lifetimes."

This was said by a man who is no fountain of superlatives, Harry P. (Bud) Grant, Marshall's coach at the time. Grant didn't say Jim Marshall was the greatest player he ever coached. What he was saying was this: Let's agree that every play in football demands the player's ultimate outpouring of energy and will, if the game is played the way it was meant to be. Let's say every down means so much to the player that he will line up with a fever of 103 degrees or broken ribs or a flu so bad he will barf on the sidelines on every change of possession. And let's say he will still extract every ounce of joy available to him from football, year after year, and he will play at championship levels for his whole career.

"What we've just done is to define Jim Marshall," Grant will you. "He was a phenomenon. There's no other way to say it."

But Grant allowed himself the storyteller's license. He did find another way. The year was 1976. The Vikings had beaten the Rams a few days before. "To understand the kind of game he played against the Rams," Grant said, "you would have to sit in our film room. You'd see a thirty-eight year old man going full bore from start to finish against one of the best teams in football, and not only against the man assigned to block him. They had a rookie quarterback [Pat Haden] so they gave him maximum protection by doubling on our defensive ends. They had a 270-pound tackle and a 230-pound fullback blocking on Marshall. I don't know how many times he shook those blocks and ran the width of the field chasing a play. You have to be in football to know how much that takes out of a man. We substituted for practically everybody on the defensive team, but Marshall was still going wide open at the finish. Buddy Ryan, our defensive coach, has seen a lot of great players over the years. He came up to me after the game. He said, 'I can't believe this guy. I never saw anybody like him.'"

The idea of a football player who spans the generations with his unquenchable zest and his obsessions for the game may be hypothetical. But Jim Marshall is no hypothesis. He would have meant as much to the Canton Bulldogs in the 1920s as he did to the Minnesota Vikings in the '60s and '70s. So we can call this guy football's "Everyman," a symbolic part of its lineage. He connects its antique days of the midcentury and its high visibility of today. For the Minnesota Vikings, we can call him a kind of icon. We can do that if you're willing to allow this icon to turn the locker room into a stage for his sappy impersonations or whistle the Mickey Mouse song when Grant put in one more of his Boy Scout rules of behavior. But Marshall bought into those rules, and so did the others. Yet being a football star never overrode his pure, adolescent impulses to keep it a game. Everybody who played with and against him knew that. They also knew that his urges to gag it up off-stage never led him to stray from his code of professionalism. And this is what made it so profound a day for dozens of his former teammates and coaches in 1999 when the Vikings retired his jersey in a ceremony at the Metrodome. Fred Zamberletti, the only trainer the Vikings ever had, was there with them. In fact, he had to be. Zamberletti was still the trainer, his place with the Vikings as indestructible as

Marshall's. In his nearly 40 years has the healer and den mother to two generations of Viking players, Zamberletti had nursed hundreds of them through fractures, sprains, muscle pulls, fright and hypochondria.

Marshall was the patient he'd never forget. He treated Marshall, all right, but it was always a little like kids playing doctor. Zamberletti knew Marshall was going to play on Sunday so he never really had to cure him. All he had to do was listen sympathetically to Marshall emitting the groans of the doomed. He also knew that if Marshall had a temperature or trench mouth or whatever was the grief of the week, he was going to play a helluva game on Sunday. It was Marshall's antidote to pain or misery.

Surrounding Freddie the day of the jersey retirement were the Vikings of 1999, who were going to play a game in a few minutes. Which meant the Viking heritage and its family—if that's what it had become—was now full, 1961 to the next millennium, joined by the crowd. Marshall stood in the center of it, his eyes touched by the memories and by his pride. The affection of his peers of 30 years ago was real. And yet it was matched by the respect and brotherhood reflected in the faces of the Viking team in uniform that day. Most of them had never seen Marshall play. But they heard all about him, his durability and his spirit and what he'd overcome.

I treasured it that way, partly because millions in the TV audience now knew something of Jim Marshall. I knew him well. We almost died together in a mountain blizzard on a snowmobile trek over the Beartooth Pass en route to Yellowstone.

One of Jim's make-believe lives in his childhood imaginings was the life of a mountaineer. Often after practices he would grill me with questions about mountaineering, about climbing in the mountains and motoring through their high snows. During the season of 1970 I told him that I was planning to organize a snowmobile run through the Beartooth Mountains of Wyoming and Montana and over the Beartooth's 11,000-foot summit ridge pass. I said he was welcome to join us. The subject didn't come up again until mop-up Monday after the Viking season ended in the playoffs. I dropped by Marshall's locker to wish him well over the off-season.

"My man," he said, "I want to go on the snowmobile trip." He did. He was joined by Paul Dickson, also a Viking defensive lineman. There were 16 of us. Late arrivals included a photographer Marshall had retained to film the event for his growing audiences.

The winds struck late in the afternoon. The day and the trip were intended simply as a romp in the snow. The day turned into a horror. The storm disabled our machines. We were spread across the mountain's summit ridge in the snow and darkness. I was with four others just below the summit. Marshall and Dickson were with another group of five 2,000 feet below us on the other side of the summit. Just before dawn of the next day, an extraordinary and gentle man, Hugh Galusha, died in a shallow snow trench where he and two others sought safety. The rest of us survived. Marshall and Dickson built a fire in the pines near one of the frozen lakes. To start it, Jim would say later, he burned $100 bills. He may have, although the chaos of the night might have been too wild to make out the denominations, or if, in fact, they were actually blank checks.

It didn't matter. He came out of it. The memory of that night will connect us for as long as we live, and we understand that with mutual fondness, although we go years now without crossing paths. When we do, it's always a good and strong reunion.

And the next season after the blizzard he was back on the line of scrimmage.

So we can legitimately call this man a football icon. We can also call him a comedian and a philosopher and chaser of the far horizons as a child of the ghetto. He looked at the world, and still does, with inquisitive big eyes and the wonderment of a man whose football career and his entire life put him on his own Yellow Brick Road each day. He was and is a man with the restless feet of Marco Polo and the mischief of an elf. If you played defensive end in the National Football League for two decades, in four Super Bowls and in the Pro Bowl, the world clearly will call you a professional. But I'm not sure the word mattered much to Jim Marshall.

The football field was his playground when the day was laced with good vibes, and his sanctuary when he was troubled. No matter his moods and his later struggles with money or drugs, the constant in his life was football. Yes, he was a professional on Sunday and all of the days of the week preceding it. But he would have played football without a payday. Because he was never very adroit about managing money, there were years when he almost did.

For as long as he played it, football was life and renewal. It seasoned each day with the potions of competition and fraternity. It was hell-raising in the locker room. It was Sunday afternoon, coming off the ball, rushing the quarterback, going after him shoulder to shoulder with Alan Page and Carl Eller, arm-fighting the blockers. It was the crowd roaring and guys on the sideline screaming, "Way to go, Big D."

He could hear Joe Kapp's voice. It always sounded as though it were coming out of a sulfur pit. "Get me that seed," Kapp was yelling. "Get me the ball." Marshall could see the blood on Kapp's jaw and even wearing his helmet you could see Joe's stitches from the day when somebody carved him up with a broken beer bottle in a bar fight in Canada. And they would come off the field together after making one more stop on defense, Marshall, Alan, Carl, Gary Larsen, Wally Hilgenberg, Paul Krause, Lonnie Warwick and the others. Grant was standing there, stationary and mute in his lumberjack mackinaw and his headset. His face was marbled with frost. Looking at him, you'd swear he'd just lost his best hunting dog instead of watching the Lions go three-and-out against the best defense in football. Still, Marshall always found that picture of Grant the Monument oddly comforting. It meant they were winning and the world was in synch.

Grant never patted your butt after you stopped the other team's offense. That didn't bother Marshall. He had an understanding with Grant. Marshall played every game to the max. It didn't matter that he weighed 230 pounds and the people across the line usually weighed 260 and 270. Marshall played on speed, instinct and something close to the moves of a cobra. Grant acknowledged that with deadpan approval. He avoided surface praise that might wash off on the team's veterans.

Once in a while Marshall would tell himself, "Hey, what's wrong with surface praise?" But Grant admired Jim and didn't have to express it constantly. In different ways, he admired Alan Page, Carl Eller, Krause, Yary, Ed White and later Tarkenton and Chuck Foreman and Ahmad Rashad. Still, Marshall remembers today, nobody who played D for the Vikings in those years demonstrated coming off the field so that you could notice. Their game face was to come off looking grim and satisfied, not exactly like the hangman leaving the scaffold but something close to that. The crowd, of course, was high-fiving everything in sight and chanting, "Kill, Carl, kill." And Marshall could see that some of the goofballs in the galleries were shirtless in the -15 wind-chill. And then Jim Marshall would tell himself, "What the hell, this is fun." So he would clap Eller on the shoulder and break out into a grin that spread from Cedar Avenue to the Viking longboat parked in the snowdrifts outside the Met. And he'd start laughing at the shirtless wonders. Grant would look quizzically in Marshall's direction and Marshall would cuff him on the shoulder and say, "Hey, Bud, isn't this the nuts?"

Bud might smile at that, but probably not. Hilarity was not a hot commodity on the Viking bench. But Grant never objected when Marshall was called on in an interview to describe what made Grant a winner. Grant's ego was as wide as most of the egos you'll find in big-time competition. It just wasn't as visible.

In his childhood, when Jim Marshall had nothing and had no prospects of making a mark, he created fantasy worlds for himself. He saw himself as a deep sea diver, as an astronaut, a daring parachutist, an explorer or a mountain climber. Whenever I wrote about those imaginary lives, Marshall would enter a mild denial. "That's you talkin'," he'd say. "I didn't have all those fantasies. You're the guy who's doing the imagining."

But I wasn't. One of the most powerful motivations that gripped him from adolescence on was to succeed in football not only to make a life for Jim Marshall, but to fulfill some of those lives from his childhood. And much of them he did. And one of those was Jim Marshall, Tamer of the Jungle. He never did get there to find The Graveyard of Elephants, but he knew who he wanted on the scene if the big man-eaters came after him.

"When I got older and some of those things started opening for me," he said, "I'd think, what if I ever got lost in the jungle? Who would I want with me if the place was crawling with crocodiles and lions and pythons? I'd think, Old Bud, there, he's the guy. If anybody was tough enough and knew where he was going every step of the way and had a cold-blooded streak in him, Bud was the guy. If anybody could get you out of that mess, Bud Grant could."

Every time he told that story, Jim would make a jester's face as though telling the listener that all of this was in good fun and he didn't really mean the part about Bud being cold-blooded.

But he probably did mean it, in the way the ballplayer would understand. Grant cut through sentimentality and alibis and didn't blow smoke, whether he was firing a player or indulging a convoluted question from the press. He didn't use insults to squelch the interrogator. He just stared, which was usually a tougher squelch than sarcasm. Loyalty was something else. He would carry a veteran a year past his prime out of loyalty. He would also carry a faltering rookie if the rookie had a chance and he worked and he listened. But fundamentally, Grant projected the personal warmth of an alligator. His players respected him because he never elevated himself at their expense. He almost never embarrassed an erring player publicly, and he seemed to his players to have his values in order. Other coaches, including some good ones, would eat themselves up in their obsession to win, haul a cot in their stadium office and sleep there. Grant went home at 5 o'clock every day. After games on Sunday, he'd go home and eat ice cream with the family and play pool with the kids.

If Grant was a stoic, Marshall, of course, was his cartoonist. When Marshall made one of those faces, he lit me up. The face of football? Sure. It was mustached and rubbery. It was one of those faces where the forces of reality and tomfoolery seem to be colliding. You could put a helmet and birdcage over Marshall's face before practice and his eyes would roll and he'd mug hugely. He could mimic anything in sight. Midweek was playtime. The locker room was playtime. There he could howl and strut. He had appreciative audiences. Ballplayers. Who else?

And was there anything more restorative and so full of electricity than the football field in the middle of the fall? Everybody hunkering on the line of scrimmage, some assistant coach bitching about spacing, Jerry Burns moaning about the offense's timing. And someplace on the roof of the baseball dugouts at scruffy Met Stadium, some birds decide to sing in the middle of practice and Marshall felt so good he joined them.

What's the deal about a hereafter, where there is glory and euphoria for saved souls? Why not have it now?

It had been years since he thought about the ugliest day of his football life, the one at Kezar in San Francisco when he picked up a 49er fumble and sprinted toward the goal line. He was running full throttle and he couldn't see Francis trying to overtake him along the sideline, yelling. Marshall was going into the end zone all right, but it wasn't the one he wanted. He'd gotten confused in the swirl of the play and ran the wrong way.

And San Francisco's Bruce Bosley chased him all the way to the end line, tapped his shoulder and said, "Nice goin', Jim, you just scored two points for us."

It was early in the national television of football, 1964. But millions saw it on the screen. For days the radio shows and round tables were full of horse laughs, all directed at the aimless professional football player who needed a compass more than shoulder pads.

Some of the comedians dug into his history. Hey, this guy needed more than a compass. He needed a portable medical clinic. He was the man who swallowed a grape the wrong way a few years before, nearly suffocated and wound up in intensive care.

And didn't this guy accidentally shoot himself admiring his revolver in his car?

The same.

The conclusion was clear. Here was one those hapless characters who'd find a way to walk under falling anvils and black clouds. Or maybe he was just naturally a klutz.

He was a long way from that. Jim Marshall did dabble in the zodiac here and there and he might have loused up his planetary alignments while he was doing it. But something fascinating and somewhat wonderful happened to him after the wrong-way run.

In the Viking locker room after the game—which the Vikings won, incidentally—I approached him, offered commiseration and said the world was going to keep spinning. "You're big enough to handle it," I said. If he felt any consolation from that it didn't register in those somber and lifeless eyes. He looked and sounded like a man in shock.

His normal personality was full of sparks and whims and the comic's caricatures. On the good days football was a celebration. On the best day it made him almost invincible.

But Sunday afternoons were also serious stuff. Football gave him dignity. The way he played it and the respect he drew from it made him feel that Jim Marshall mattered. When he and his team played it right, the crowd at home roared its gratification and sent his adrenaline surging like a runaway river. Sure it was just a game. The metaphors about it, "war in the trenches," were rhetoric, and overdrawn rhetoric at that. But the battle was real. It produced real heroes. Marshall wanted to be one of those. Often he was. But that afternoon at Kezar drained all of his dignity, all of the worth he'd battled to build. That ideal sustained him through his siege of encephalitis and weight loss that led the Cleveland Browns to trade him to Minnesota after his rookie season. He fought through a form of sleeping sickness. Some days he played defensive end in the National Football League weighing 210 pounds. Even healthy, he'd lose 10 or 15 pounds during the season. The Viking years, particularly the Grant years, were so heady for him there were times when Jim Marshall decided that it was in the cards for him to play football forever. He came closer than most.

But this was the locker room at Kezar and he wanted to crawl behind the

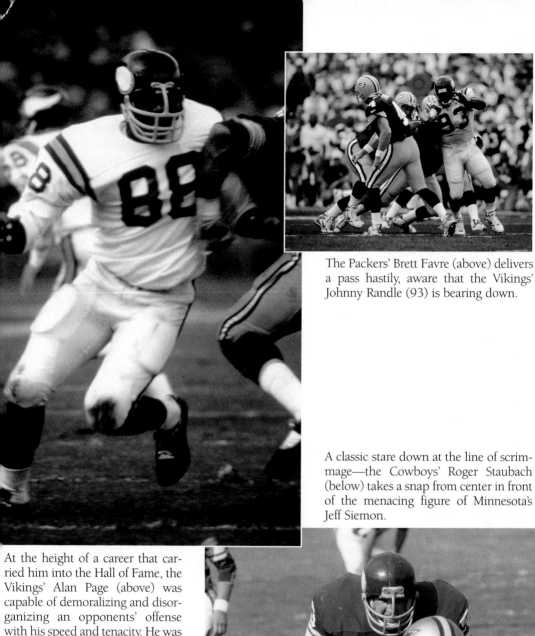

The Packers' Brett Favre (above) delivers a pass hastily, aware that the Vikings' Johnny Randle (93) is bearing down.

A classic stare down at the line of scrimmage—the Cowboys' Roger Staubach (below) takes a snap from center in front of the menacing figure of Minnesota's Jeff Siemon.

At the height of a career that carried him into the Hall of Fame, the Vikings' Alan Page (above) was capable of demoralizing and disorganizing an opponents' offense with his speed and tenacity. He was the first defensive lineman named the NFL's Most Valuable Player.

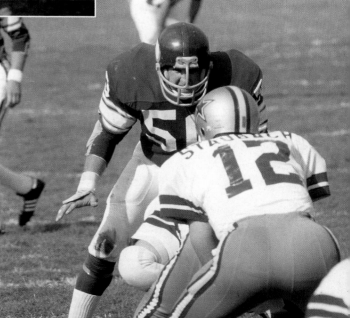

In the early 1960s, the Vikings' Fran Tarkenton became the prototype of what football people now call a "mobile" quarterback. In Tarkenton's years he was called a scrambler and names less polite by panting defensive linemen who had to chase him. Tarkenton ultimately appeared in three Super Bowls, threw 340 touchdown passes and was named to the Hall of Fame.

Tarkenton never gave up on a broken play. Here he throws on the run against Tampa Bay.

Nobody wrote hymns to the quarterbacking artistry of Joe Kapp (11), the Vikings' first Super Bowl quarterback. Joe was a grunt and a brawler whose forward passes flopped around but usually got there. His teammates loved his roughshod style, and he won with it. At right, he unloads a pass through the arms of a leaping defender. In 1969 Kapp tied a record with seven touchdown passes in one game.

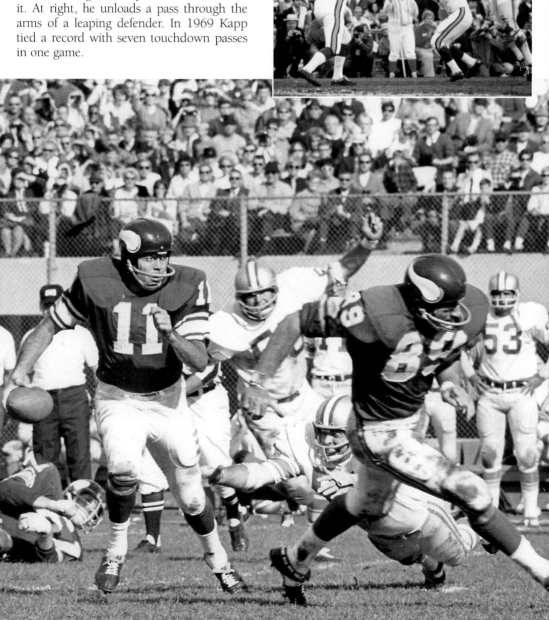

The Vikings' first coach, the turbulent Norm Van Brocklin (above, white shirt), was drawn to big farm kids who liked to mix it up. Mick Tingelhoff (53) was one of the rough treasures of the Vikings' early years, a free agent center from Nebraska who was the team's first All-Pro. Monte Kiffin (56), now an NFL assistant coach, and John Kirby also played for Nebraska.

On the sidelines, Bud Grant (left) was always sartorially practical. When the north winds and the snow came, Grant donned his fur-collared coat, jammed his headset over his ear and told his players "we win in lousy weather." Mostly, they did.

Jerry Burns (above) could snarl and curse, but he was essentially a likeable guy with a restless coaching mind who devised imaginative offenses and nearly took the Vikings to a Super Bowl.

Les Steckel (above) was the Viking head coach for one forgetable season when they won just three games. He was an ex-Marine whose military disciplines just didn't work. Later as an NFL coaching assistant, he mellowed and achieved success.

Dennis Green (right) arrived in the early 90s as "the new sheriff in town." Despite an impressive eight-year winning record, the 2000 season was generally recognized as the High Noon for the sheriff, a make-or-break season.

Cris Carter's one hand catch against the Packers dramatically explains why the Vikings' veteran receiver was named to the NFL's Team of the 90s. He entered the 2000 season having caught 114 touchdown passes, a mark which with all of his other statistics and his vast prestige in the NFL put him squarely on the road to pro football's Hall of Fame.

In his early seasons, Cris Carter's life was in disarray. He was addicted to chemicals and was dumped by the Philadelphia Eagles. But in Minnesota he came to grips with his dependency, found spiritual peace and now carries that message wherever he goes.

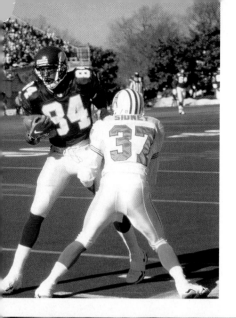

They were calling Randy Moss (84) the wonder child of pro football after his fifth game. After his first season, they were calling him an All-Pro. He could outleap three defenders at a time and outrun anybody still standing. He was swift, versatile, cocksure and on some days immature. But he could score each time he touched the ball. At left, he fakes out a defensive back. At right, Moss is poised to go one-on-one against a cornerback. Below, he outruns the Chicago Bears behind a Cris Carter block.

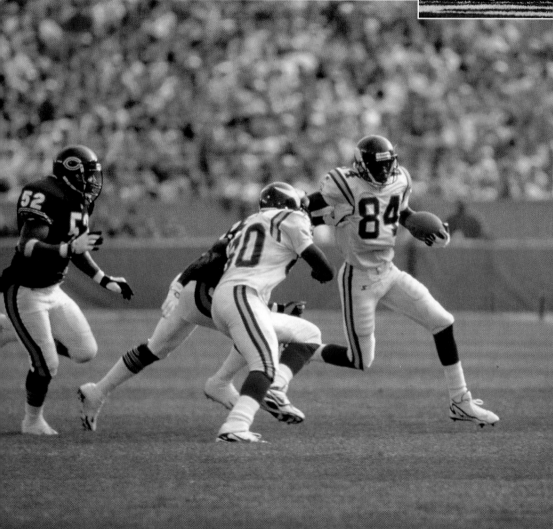

Everybody but the Vikings ignored Johnny Randle (left) at recruiting time. He had injuries and no big deeds in college. But he became the most respected defensive tackle of the decade in the NFL, and loved the locker-room banter almost as much as the action.

The most memorable single image of the Viking years at the Metropolitan Stadium was Bud Grant, standing in the snowflakes, phone set on his head, silently in command. The guy never blinked—and rarely lost.

When the Vikings' Robert Smith (right) sees daylight, the end zone is never far away. With his long stride, his track speed and his breakout ability, Smith is one of the ranking runners in football.

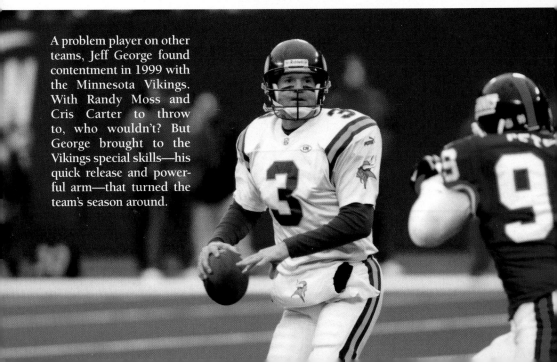

A problem player on other teams, Jeff George found contentment in 1999 with the Minnesota Vikings. With Randy Moss and Cris Carter to throw to, who wouldn't? But George brought to the Vikings special skills—his quick release and power-ful arm—that turned the team's season around.

blocking dummies. That was his place. Nobody would recognize him there. It's where he belonged. With the dummies. It's what he felt. But what he heard was a newspaper writer asking him a favor. "Jimbo," I said. "We've got a football luncheon Mondays at the Nicollet Hotel in Minneapolis. I'd like you to be my guest for a short interview. I know you feel lousy right now, but people forgive. It might be good for you." He stared at me as though I was about to hand him a subpoena. "You got to be kidding. I'm going to stand up and let hundred people laugh at me?"

"Four hundred," I said. "And they're not going to laugh at you. They're decent folks. You'll be welcome."

I wouldn't have asked him that if I didn't believe it.

He showered, talked to a couple of San Francisco reporters between his long and pained silences, and came back to his locker. "OK," he said, "I'll be there."

At 10:30 the next morning in Minneapolis I got a phone call from him. "I'm sorry to tell you this," he said, "but I changed my mind. I don't want to put myself through that. Maybe another time."

I asked him not to hang up. He didn't. He didn't want to renege but the embarrassment was eating him up. We talked for 10 minutes. He said finally, "OK." When he entered the banquet hall a few minutes late, I introduced him as he was walking to the head table, and 400 people stood up and applauded. The reception was noisy and congenial. Marshall smiled for the first time in two days. We bantered at the microphone for half an hour. The questions from the crowd were endless but friendly, and when Marshall left the luncheon he did it with the step of a man with fresh good news from the doctor: The condition wasn't terminal after all.

The wrong-way run might have destroyed him. It would have if he'd allowed the inevitable ridicule to turn his embarrassment into a poison of resentment and withdrawal. What he did was to join the laughter when some emcee brought it up at a nightclub, and to play better football the rest of the season than he ever had. And within a year or two, not many people around the country remembered who it was who ran the wrong way in San Francisco, and a year or so after that, nobody cared.

I watched the ceremony on my TV the day they retired his number at the Metrodome in 1999. From the couch in my workroom den I joined the applause. Before it was over, my eyes were pretty well fogged up. Here was a marvelous football player for whom the game was a jubilee almost every day. But he'd overcome. He'd overcome illnesses and a dozen injuries and later he'd overcome chemicals and the oblivion where drugs had led him for a while. And his response to his loss of public visibility in his retirement was to discover yet another Jim Marshall, who didn't need the applause and later the highs to renew himself. This Jim Marshall didn't need to make a mark. What he needed and wanted was to find kids who needed a friend. So he became a friend, working with them on playgrounds and schools, in the neighborhoods and the ghetto.

He still does. Yet my applause was not only for that. Seeing the fondness in the eyes of all of the players around him, players now in their 60s and players in their 20s, I remembered the night we almost died together in the mountain blizzard, and I remembered one other day. The Vikings had beaten Cleveland to win the National Football League title in January of 1970. They were going to the Super Bowl. And in the middle of their boisterous locker room, streamers of white tape were flying off the walls and ceiling and bedlam was not far behind. Coagulated blood caked the face of the quarterback, Joe Kapp. Carl Eller and Jim Marshall peeled the dead grass and mud off their arms. Kapp lifted a bottle of champagne triumphantly over his head and waved it in the direction of Eller and Marshall. And Eller yelled, "Hey, Joe. Joe Kapp. You're our brother, man." The three of them advanced through the falling tape and their bellowing teammates. They hugged each other mightily, two African-Americans and a Hispanic, affirming the bond of battle, their shared commitment and, at this exultant moment, their love.

Sitting in my home applauding Jim Marshall's last hurrah in the autumn of 1999, I lifted that locker-room scene out of 30 years ago and I allowed myself a harmless reverie. Here was a moment that elevated a game, professional football, to a place that deserved the passion and the energy of those who watch it. It redeemed the violence and huge money and the television frenzy devoted to it.

If pro football could produce that locker-room scene at the Met 30 years ago and if the Jim Marshall of 1999 could connect the eras of the game so simply and believably, then he might have been right in one of his fantasies.

Maybe he *is* football forever.

"All he can do is catch passes
in the end zone."

—Buddy Ryan's mysterious judgment of Cris Carter's
pro football capabilities when he released him
in Philadelphia early in Carter's career.

Again–The Dogged Pursuit of Futility and the Super Bowl– Starring Cris Carter

Dec. 26, 1999

When you see a man noodling around among the ghosts and legends of his 43 years in newspapering, you are seeing a man who has cordially accepted his fate as an ancient minstrel. Which I have done. You may have noticed. It's a life that presents no danger to society. The minstrel's stories are harmless. Some of them may even approach the borders of entertainment.

But at this moment I'm glancing at the calendar on my wall and the date reads Dec. 26, 1999. All ghosts I'd planned to invoke today have disappeared because here comes The Prophet flying into my television screen on a Sunday afternoon. He jolts me out of my reveries and the aromas of Palmer Pyle's lasagna of 35 years ago. The Prophet, Cris Carter, is the here-and-now of football and he is one prophet who does not deal in white beards and robes. What he is doing is kicking butt in the New York Giants' secondary. The Prophet is on a crusade and, although he is described as being somewhat lame with a sprained ankle, he is unstoppable. Before he's finished on Dec. 26, 1999, the Vikings will have made it to the National Football Conference playoffs and Carter is not surprised.

He predicted it. He practically demanded it. He is an ordained minister and therefore passable as a prophet. He is a reverend with an ego in high gear on the football field, a laser temper, a bellyacher about bad calls and he is armed with rough-and-tumble elbows that often find their way into a cornerback's gut. But to his team, his coach and the grunts on the other side of the line of scrimmage he is utterly believable because on this day, Dec. 26, 1999, he may be the best football player in the world–and had been all year.

Suddenly on this day, no matter what would happen down the road, the ages for me were improbably fused, the grail reappeared: the Vikings and the Super Bowl.

Again.

"God," the minstrel sighed. Here it is. One more time. The Vikings-and-the-Super Bowl is one of those sagas of human futility almost too grievous to record. It is a medieval morality play that seems never to end. You could more sensibly call it the Vikings versus the Super Bowl. For 30 years this organization had lusted after the mountaintop experience of the football cosmos. And each time it had disappeared ingloriously into a crevasse, swallowed whole.

Nonetheless, the battered old forbidden dream was unleashed. Were the Vikings ever going to win the Super Bowl? Is there a rose garden at the North Pole? Four times the Minnesota Vikings had played in the Super Bowl. Four times they blew it. I'd reported them all. When I came back from New Orleans or Houston or Pasadena, I got telephone calls by the truckload. Why can't these guys win the Super Bowl? Most of these I fended off manfully. I said it wasn't that they can't. They just haven't. This was not a very majestic explanation, I admit. One of the callers irritated me and I called him a mindless jerk. He said he knew my route to and from work and he'd by laying for me tomorrow night. I said if his maps weren't any better than his logic, I was safe.

But before The Prophet came, that was the Super Bowl syndrome in Minnesota. Thousands of people actually believed it was some kind of curse laid on 4.5 million people by an unreasonable providence. Minnesota was the place where nobody won the big one and Minnesota was destined to be No. 2 wherever it went. Hubert Humphrey and Walter Mondale lost in presidential elections. Minnesota was runner-up to Wisconsin in cheese and to somebody else in corn and oats. Minnesota led in taconite, but how many people in Japan could spell "taconite"? Even our blizzards lagged behind North Dakota's in wind-chill. The Twins finally broke the curse by winning the World Series in 1987 and 1991 but the football multitudes weren't appeased.

In 1998 this was a football team that was loaded with premium players who were probably the best in football compositely. They came within one last-second field goal of reaching the Super Bowl. They should have been there. But they weren't. Not many in their audience in Minnesota called that the Super Bowl curse. They called it a choke. Football fans who are denied are not the most merciful folk. And so when the 1999 season slipped into disarray, the bafflement and contempt of the minions got deeper. The Vikings lost four of their first six games. Why? For one, the quarterback, Randall Cunningham, had lost his guru, Brian Billick, who'd become the head coach in Baltimore. To Cunningham, Billick's replacement, Ray Sherman, seemingly felt strange and unhelpful. And this decent and God-fearing athlete who'd received all the adulation the year before, Cunningham, looked oddly disoriented and indecisive. The Vikings lost. Todd Steussie and some of the others slumped along with Cunningham. The Vikings lost. Moss sulked when he wasn't in the middle of the action or snagging touchdown passes one-handed with three defensive backs draped on his shoulders. The Vikings' young secondary went south. And they lost.

In the middle of their fourth loss, in Detroit, Dennis Green, the coach, replaced Cunningham with Jeff George. The Viking offense stabilized. The fans decided grudgingly that Sherman was acceptable. Cris Carter stepped into all remaining voids and pushed the Vikings into a winning streak. But they lost successive games to Tampa Bay and Kansas City and the curse was back because Carter went down with an ankle sprain in Kansas City. The curse expanded. Their record read 7 wins, 6 losses. The fans wallowed in depression. These guys are going into the tank again, they moaned. They're as lousy as the rest of the league.

They weren't. They still had some of the best players in football, not all of them playing at their 1998 form, but forming a team that had the armament to reach the Super Bowl. Cris Carter knew that. Yes, there was the defense. Apart from Johnny Randle, the line was ordinary and even Randle was less than he'd been. Most days, the pass-rush was negligible. Eddie McDaniel and Dwayne Rudd were quality linebackers. Yet Rudd seemed ordinary most games and the defensive backs were vulnerable. On some days they were pure and simply terrible. Whose weren't? For most of the season the Vikings had only one dependable man in the secondary, Robert Griffith, the sledgehammer safety. The free agency loss of Corey Fuller, the fiasco of Ramos McDonald, who was dumped in midseason, the injury to Orlando Thomas and the off year of Jimmy Hitchcock meant that the Viking secondary had to undergo a new incarnation each month. In the end the Vikings had to recreate the wide receiver Robert Tate, and turned him into a defensive back in the teeth of the season's crisis.

Yet it wasn't until months later that the Viking public learned about the fallout from that rocky beginning of the 1999 season and the internal bad blood that may have instigated it. Twin Cities newspapers, the St. Paul

Pioneer Press and the Minneapolis *Star Tribune*, in March published dark sagas of players confronting players behind closed locker-room doors. In stories written by veteran reporters Don Banks in St. Paul and Kent Youngblood in Minneapolis, they told of accusations against Cris Carter for laying blame on some of his teammates both privately and publicly. They learned of alleged shouting and physical shoving matches between assistant coach Richard Solomon and defensive back Ramos McDonald. They read of prolonged bitterness of some of the Viking defensive veterans directed at Dennis Green's decision to pass up the highly-rated defensive lineman, Jevon Kearse, in the 1999 draft of college players in favor of quarterback Daunte Culpepper, who would predictably be of no help in the Vikings' 1999 bid for a Super Bowl championship. The publicly-identified sources for most of these and other charges were cornerback Jimmy Hitchcock and defensive end Duane Clemons, both of whom were cut loose by the Vikings a few weeks earlier.

Claims of team discord made by discontented players are common currency in professional athletics, or any athletics, for that matter. This does not mean the facts in the accusations were inaccurate, all or in part. It does mean the weight given to them by the unhappy informers may have been a stretch. Random intramural squabbling is usually a fact of life among highly paid and self-centered athletes looking out for their own careers in the context of a team game. But Hitchcock and Clemons were suggesting something deeper than surface incidents such as an alleged flare-up between Robert Smith, the cerebral running back, and Randy Moss over the volume of Moss' locker-room stereo. It was presumably deeper, also, than the encounter between Solomon and McDonald.

They were talking about a season-long resentment over Green's draft decisions and Green's refusal to give the respected veteran, Randall McDaniel, a more pricey contract than his current one, a promise made in the late-'90s by the Vikings' then-director of contract negotiations, Jeff Diamond. Hitchcock was saying further that many of the players resented Solomon's handling of McDonald, the young cornerback whose gaffes on the field infuriated Solomon to the point where, Hitchcock implied, the defensive back's coach was conducting a reign of terror against the young player. McDonald was dropped from the team before the end of the season.

There was more. Solomon and Green have been close for years. Not only the players but the rest of the coaching assistants were clearly aware of that relationship in any of their dealings with Solomon. Coaching assistants and players alike were said to be worried about their words or opinions, if heard or known by Solomon, getting back to Green.

There was still more. Carter's habit of functioning as the team warden and overseer of professionalism on the field grated on some of the players, although their respect for his abilities and his right to the role of team leader was unquestioned. In the first Green Bay game, Hitchcock was beaten on a pass play that cost the Vikings the game in the late moments. Television cameras caught Carter upbraiding Hitchcock on the sidelines. In the subsequent team meeting Hitchcock confronted Carter, saying the star receiver had to come down from his loftiness and talk and act on the same level as the other players. Without accusing Carter, Jerry Ball said the finger-pointing had to stop. Carter said he had apologized to Hitchcock and insisted his outburst was not personal, but he did criticize the way Randall Cunningham and McDonald were playing, according to one of the Vikings who attended the meeting. Chris Doleman defended Carter, and attributed the incident to Carter's competitiveness. "As if we aren't all competitive," a player commented.

And finally, Viking players told of a loss of the camaraderie of the 1998 season, due in part to owner Red McCombs' promotion of Green to the dual role of coach and de facto general manager. It meant Green not only handled the team on the field but negotiated with them on salary, which some of the players found intimidating. And some of them appeared wary of Carter's confidential status with Green, which they regarded as a role that made Cris a kind of management advocate in the locker room.

So did all of this truly constitute some kind of cancer eroding the unity of the team and the mutual respect between players and coaches, particularly the players and Green?

It probably did. To what degree that affected the team's play is pure conjecture. After losing 4 of their first 6 games, and after the team meeting, the Vikings won 8 out of their next 10 behind the quarterbacking of Jeff George, who replaced Cunningham at quarterback. That hardly has the look of a team bristling with dissension. The offensive line, in disarray early in the season, played to its 1998 level. The aerial carnival of George, Carter and Moss destroyed the league's defenses. Hitchcock played hard, if below his 1998 form. The defense, though, never mended and got flattened by St. Louis in the midplayoffs.

The general uprooting of the Viking coaching assistants when the season ended was a symptom of some of the internal frictions. Solomon's status wasn't touched. Was all of the tension and squabbling any different from what most quality teams go through when they fall short of a goal? Probably not. Was it a reason the team fell short of that goal? It probably was, but not as important a reason as the team's defensive mediocrity, which was partly Green's responsibility from his decisions in the draft and partly the price of the Vikings' 1998 success, and the free agent losses the salary cap cost them.

Despite their midseason revival, Vikings were within one loss in December of disappearing and the reverend was walking around in a cast. Somebody thought there was a chance he wouldn't play again in 1999. At least that was the ominous news wafting around the sports pages and talk shows and from the locker room. Cris Carter didn't exactly discourage those reports but he and his coach did suggest that if anybody could play with that injury, Cris Carter would and could.

Prophets deal in miracles. Give them room.

So here came the reverend, just two weeks after a serious ankle sprain, running his routes against the Giants' banged-up and befuddled defensive backs and actually outrunning them.

In just three hours, he relit the torch of hope for his football team and its white-knuckled followers. It's what prophets do.

He didn't do it by himself. This was a football team that a year before had 10 people playing in the Pro Bowl, meaning all of them were chosen by their peers as the best at their position or near the best. That is a vast number. It was a team that included the football prodigy, Randy Moss, casually haughty and sometimes indifferent but graced with unlimited gifts and capable personally of destroying any pass defense on any day or on any play—if he felt moved to behave professionally on that particular day. It included Jeff George, the cannon-armed quarterback resurrected in midseason from a past of failure and unpopularity. In the pits there was Johnny Randle, the happy blabbermouth who was still one of the better defensive linemen in football; Randall McDaniel, no blabbermouth but also a veteran lineman of achievement; Robert Smith, a marvelous runner when healthy; Eddie McDaniel and Rudd at linebacker; Jeff Christie, Todd Steussie and Korey Stringer on the offensive line; and Mitch Berger, the best punter and kickoff man in pro football. And more.

Their coach, Dennis Green, was largely unloved by the paying public in the stadium or by the throngs in front of their TVs. A couple of years before, he'd written an angry and misguided book threatening to sue his own management for a part of the financial action. At the time it seemed closer to an act of professional suicide than any serious attempt to redress an injustice that was never clear to the public or to the owners. He'd been involved in a mysterious court case that developed around an alleged abusive relationship. It dragged for months and eventually came to nothing, but it tended to discredit him with the public. Until he underwent a remarkable streamlining in 1998 with the loss of 60 or 70 pounds, he was the fat guy on the Viking sidelines with very meager appeal to the viewing public. And he was no politician. Few media people got close to him or were allowed to. In the midst of his troubles he issued prepared statements or TV bites, some of which seemed to originate from a private bunker, geography unknown. He trusted almost nobody in the media business and reflexively raised stone walls to their overtures.

For most of his tenure as the Viking coach, which began in 1992, he was an irresistible target for headhunters in the opinion columns. His teams won most of the time, and they reached the playoffs almost all of the time, but they never reached very far. Worse, they seemed to reserve some of their least inspirational football for the playoffs, and in a couple of games they looked absolutely lousy.

From the beginning, I thought Green was a quality coach. In the expanding age of million dollar players, players who increasingly held the coach hostage with their big salaries and free agency options, Green's teams revealed few if any symptoms of unrest. The prima donnas among his stars continued to be prima donnas, but they uniformly played up to or close to their capabilities for him. Most of them respected him and in ways available to them, they let the public know that. Some of them adopted his clenched-teeth attitude toward media people, but there was no discernible warfare between the two. He was one of the pioneering black coaches in football and he vocally campaigned for more, which seemed to bring the African-Americans on his team closer and gave no cause to bother the whites. With some exceptions, his teams seemed to present a workaday discipline absent from many of their rivals. He also understood personnel as well as most and better than some.

His decision to squander his two first-round choices in the 1999 draft on unknown commodities, unusable in 1999, attracted early flak from the critics and should have. With the great college pass-rusher, Jevon Kearse, available as the 11th choice on the first round, Green rejected the advice of most of his coaches and picked Daunte Culpepper, a big quarterback from a small school, who early on revealed absolutely no readiness to help the team in 1999 and wasn't drafted for that purpose. Green's second first-round choice, Michigan State defensive lineman Dimitrius Underwood, was a catastrophe. He wouldn't play in his final year at Michigan State, for mysterious reasons the State coaches never fathomed. Further, the State coaches couldn't see any reason why he'd play for the pros, either. Green thought he would respond to the Viking environment and that he had huge potential. Underwood fled after one day in camp to follow, he said, God. A few weeks later, he tried to cut his throat in despondency. He was an emotionally troubled young man with a history that should have raised powerful warning flags. But Green had been right on Moss the year before. So he drafted Underwood and got zero contributions from the first round, and no help for a limping defense.

Yet Green had succeeded with his hunches after Moss. Most coaches passed on Jeff George after the 1998 season when his $4 million salary gave out in Oakland. George was a loser, a loner and a probable troublemaker. He also insisted he was still a No. 1 quarterback. Green gave him a proposition. With a lot of teams, Green agreed, you'd be No. 1. With us, you won't be unless something happens to Randall Cunningham. But we'd like to have you. We can afford $400,000 under the salary cap.

George wasn't salivating to sign right now, today, with anybody. He had money. Sooner or later somebody's No. 1 quarterback was going down in the 1999 season and George would look awfully attractive, bum reputation and all. But the Vikings were a playoff team. Green sounded sensible to him. He wasn't a charmer or a screamer but his teams won.

George signed for $400,000. He knew his skills. In a stable playing environment, if they ever gave him the ball, he could deliver.

Green saw that this was possible where most of the rest of the league didn't. The other reality was that Green had Cris Carter, Randy Moss and Jake Reed running pass routes. The others didn't. On the George decision, the grouchiest Green critics weren't able to deny the evidence: When Cunningham failed to ignite the team, the Vikings could replace him with something more than a rookie lamb or a shopworn mediocrity who would wreck their season. What they had on the bench, and now in the game, was a quarterback with some of the most refined skills in professional football.

George was No. 1 after 5½ games. From there the Vikings won 5 in a row and lost only 2 of their last 10 in the season. One reason beyond George, Carter, Johnny Randle and Robert Smith, of course, was the other player who'd come to the Vikings with a dossier red with the warning flags of trouble. Nineteen National Football League teams passed on Moss in the 1998 draft. He had a police record. It was nothing huge—possession of marijuana and assault against a high school classmate. But it did not create any lasting affection for him at Notre Dame and then Florida State. For a couple of years he was a football orphan before settling at Marshall. The pro scouts who watched him there said privately they had seen no one like him in years. He was swift, tall, almost supernaturally athletic and combative when he felt like being combative. He could step into anybody's offense in the NFL right now. But there were all of those red flags. And they remembered some of the big first-round draft choices who carried those flags and departed as busts, Lawrence Phillips and others. Green looked into Moss' delinquency record. It wasn't all that heinous. He also remembered drafting Dwayne Rudd when others wouldn't. Rudd was regarded as a risk by some of the scouts around the NFL. With the Vikings he raised no problems at all and became one of the better linebackers in football in two years. So Green drafted Moss, and the NFL came face-to-face with a legitimate superstar practically in his pro infancy. Moss' response to being drafted 21st was calm and not overly burdened with modesty. He said he wasn't mad at anybody who passed on him, but personally he would have picked Randy Moss as No. 1.

When I covered pro football for the newspaper, my season began in mid-July, tramping the sidelines of the Viking training camps and writing those endless profiles that masquerade as football news in summer. When I retired from newspapering my football season usually began in September on the upper bench of the sauna at my athletic club. It began there because most of the sauna inmates were football fans.

And the ones who were streaming sweat generally knew about my football history. This did not necessarily produce a relationship in which the kindly professor tended to the intellectual vacuums of the inquiring scholars. A fierce democracy reigned. Under the ground rules, the scholars brought knowledge to the seminar that was at least equal to the professor's, and opinions that were probably more incisive, blunt and ruthless. Here I ought to clear up a misunderstanding about football fans as an aging minstrel sees them. It's true that sometimes they bleed pure purple or blue or (it's the trend) pure black, which, incidentally, is not easy to do. But unless their team won the Super Bowl the previous year, they tend mostly to be frosty pes-

simists, shorn of all reasonable hope and convinced, even in September, that their football team is headed for oblivion, again. The same old story.

The inquiring scholar in midseason was a sleek, bald man of middle age who'd been spinning on a club bicycle. For his withdrawal exercise he decided to beat on the head of the professor.

"You've been saying here all season that the Vikings have some of the best personnel in football and ought to make it to the Super Bowl."

"I have," I said.

"Have you looked at the standings? They're muddling. Their defense is lousy."

"That's mostly right," I said. "They still have the best team in the Central Division and should make the playoffs. If they do that they have the team to reach the Super Bowl."

"You've also been telling us that Denny Green is a good coach. The players relate well with him and he's made some good and risky personnel choices. How do you defend that now and do you really enjoy being in the minority all the time?"

"With you guys," I said, "anybody who tries reason is usually in the minority." I mentioned the choices of Moss, George and Rudd. I said he'd brought back Jerry Ball and Chris Doleman after the season started. I think those were major and positive decisions.

"You said good choices. So in 1999, with a team that went 15-1 last year and has a chance to get to the Super Bowl with a couple of strong draft choices, Green has two first rounders. The first one he picks is Daunte Culpepper, a quarterback who never played against big-time college competition and no way can help the team in 1999. The second one he picks is Dimitrius Underwood, a defensive end, a psyche case out of Michigan State. He plays one day in training camp and disappears. A couple of weeks later he tried to cut his throat and is never going to play a down in pro ball. That's Denny Green's harvest from the 1999 draft. What do you say to that?"

I told him I would say in October of 1999 that those seemed to be colossal blunders but it's not necessarily what we would say in January 2000. I didn't say Green was an oracle in picking players. I said he was good at it and most of his risks worked out.

"So you're still peddling this half-baked idea that the Vikings have one of the best teams in the NFL and could make it to the Super Bowl?"

I said, "With luck, yes." I added wistfully that sometimes a man feels terribly lonely being stuck with the truth.

For the beleaguered professor the truth was not that the Vikings were necessarily going to the Super Bowl but that they had the players with a very good chance of getting there, no matter their season record or Denny Green's bizarre choices in the 1999 NFL draft.

All of these meditations kept bringing me back to Carter, to the events of the Giants' game on Dec. 26 and the whirl of colliding impressions this man had created since he first arrived in Minnesota nearly a decade before, two years before Green's time in Minnesota.

We know now that Carter is headed for the pro football Hall of Fame. He is going in, clerical collar or no clerical collar. Carter as a Hall of Famer is ordained and irreversible. When you look at Carter's 13-year career and his impact on the Vikings and the National Football League, it's possible to be dazzled by the numbers and to look past something far more intriguing. And that is this man's dominating presence–close to imperial–and the extraordinary shifts in his personal history.

The numbers are arresting enough. You'll need the calculator. Only Jerry Rice has caught more than his 114 touchdown receptions. Only Rice, Lance Alworth and Tim Brown have reached or surpassed his seven straight seasons of more than 1,000 yards in pass receptions. He caught his 900th pass in November of 1999. Only Rice, Art Monk and Andre Reed had done that previously. And the arithmetic goes on.

But watching Carter on the field dissolves any need for arithmetic. Here is a football player in full and robust possession of who he is, supremely confident because no one could possibly be more prepared. His body is tuned to the violence ahead. He is a veteran but in the minutes before the game he is revved to a pitch that you usually see in the face of a high school kid pumping himself for the big game. Carter roams impetuously among his teammates. He bangs the chest of Jeff George, who doesn't always look that supercharged. "Feel it [the energy]", Carter yells. "Feel it!"

Oh, they feel it all right. When Carter tells them to feel it, they feel. No one has to tell them that here is the leader. They know it because they see a man with all of his psyche and guts and brains into the game. And the other people who better know that are the ones on the other side of the line. If they don't, Carter will hand them their heads, jocks and press clips.

But we'll back up here. Where was Cris Carter in 1990, a few weeks after catching 11 touchdown passes for the Philadelphia Eagles?

He was in football's equivalent of the junkyard, called the waiver wire. On the waiver wire for exactly $100 you could acquire a football player publicly unwanted by his previous employers. And why was Cris Carter unwanted by the Philadelphia Eagles?

"All he can do is catch passes in the end zone," snorted his coach, Buddy Ryan.

All Ernest Hemingway could do was write.

But you know, of course, that Buddy Ryan lied. Cris Carter could do more on a football field than catch touchdown passes. But what he was doing off the field was killing Ryan and possibly Carter. He was into chemicals big, and Ryan didn't know what to do about it. He liked the big, powerful kid from Ohio State, but there was no place for him on Ryan's team if Carter was going to let drugs and booze drag him and the team down.

The Vikings, then coached by Jerry Burns, had heard something about that. But they claimed Carter. One of the Viking directors was Wheelock Whitney, who had helped found the Johnson Institute for the treatment of chemical dependency. Early in Carter's stewardship he introduced the player to a dependency counselor. In the early weeks, Carter wasn't burning with fervor to give up those boosters. But the realization ultimately came. Ryan, Whitney and the counselor were right. Admit the dependency. Carter did. Stop using. Carter did. Find or rediscover a power bigger than the drugs or booze. Turn over the problem to that power.

God came back into the life of the drifting football player. Carter accepted humbly, and later with testimony and then with public celebrations. You may have noticed.

While I saw most of the Viking games at the Metrodome in those seasons, I wasn't writing football daily then and I didn't know him. His struggles were still relatively fresh, but there wasn't any question about the dynamism he was bringing to the football game. Within a couple of years he would be a Pro Bowl player. His peers were conditioned to his style, which was never to accept any yardage less than enough. He would lunge with the ball, arm outstretched, for one more yard. In time, everybody in the league was copying that move. He would smash into linebackers and defensive backs after he made the catch, look for daylight among the falling bodies or hit somebody with a forearm before going down. When Carter caught the ball, he, not the defensive back or the linebacker, was the attacker.

All of that was admirable and part of the code. Not so admirable was his yapping on the sideline when he approached an individual record and seemed to be demanding the ball in a meaningless game. Me first. It looked that way, and you were prompted to say that the reverend might profit from another look at the Beatitudes. He railed at the officials full-time or at anybody who seemed to be in the way of Cris Carter's agenda. He called that competing. It probably was. But to at least some of the old-liners, including me, he had the appearance of a self-serving football player with enormous drive and will whose act sometimes got to be a pain in the rump.

I shared that annoyance with one of the retired Vikings, a player with a reputation for being a team guy. The old pro nodded and laughed. "Yeah, he does some of those things. Being an ordained minister doesn't mean you can't be belligerent or have it figured out that what's good for me is good for the team. A lot of players feel that way. Most players aren't as vocal as Carter, excluding the trash-talkers. Carter talks trash sometimes, but it's not as dumb as most trash. [He once told a noisy cornerback who was yelling with two gold teeth in his mouth: "You ever think of getting another guy to do your dental work?"] His maturity and leadership just make him more credible when he gets pushy that way. There are a dozen ways to define a leader. Carter gives you most of them. You've got to agree he's a one-in-a-thousand football player."

The ancient minstrel deferred his grumbles. Carter was that, all right, and never more than in 1999, when he threw off a cast, made five catches and put the Vikings into the playoffs.

Someplace in the middle of that season I heard him talk to a small group of men, some of whom had fought off the booze themselves, and all of whom were serious about their spiritual lives. He acknowledged his self-destructive early life in football. He talked frankly but sympathetically about the troubles of some of the younger players today, making no judgments but making no excuses, either. He talked about his mission with kids. He talked both solemnly and joyously about his relationship with God, that it had saved his life and allowed him to enter other lives. Football didn't define him, he said. His relationship with God did. Being devout didn't mean he couldn't hammer a defensive back and yell at a teammate who screwed up, or make mistakes himself. He talked for an hour. He was utterly believable and he'd enlarged his portrait as a football star. It didn't mean he yielded his ego. I don't think you'll see much meekness from this guy. It didn't mean he'd abandoned his temper (e.g., slamming the ball to protest an official's call and accidentally bouncing it into the official's face). That'll be 15 yards for being unsportsmanlike, Reverend.

You can amend the Viking old pro's critique. Make Carter one in a few hundred thousand. We'll return to the reverend later. But after the Giants game I thumbed through my clippings of the 1999 football season, and there it was, in black and white, weeks earlier in the season. Prophets don't equivocate. The Vikings, Carter said, had the kind of team that was going for the Super Bowl and should make it.

There was a note on the clipping. Mine. It said, "I don't know if this guy is a prophet or a politician. I know he's a football player and he's right. This team has the players to go to the Super Bowl." There was another note. Mine. "It doesn't mean they're going to the Super Bowl. It just means they should."

My note said this wasn't a prophecy. It was an evaluation.

"... The next big movement... in pro football is the globalization of it... competition between American NFL teams and European and Asian NFL teams... It's inevitable... "

–Mike Lynn, visualizing pro football from Cairo to Tokyo.

Only Midas Knows How Football Works Today

*I*t took the TV masses in America months to figure out what a football derelict like Jeff George was doing running the high-octane Viking offense in 1999.

Here was a man with a reputation. This was the quarterback-in-exile of the National Football League, the man without a ball club, as popular as flu wherever he went. Wasn't that correct?

It may have been correct without being totally right. But, yes, that was a reasonably fair description of George's status in early 1999.

By the end of the year there were some NFL coaches who were calling Jeff George the best quarterback in football, allowing for Brett Favre's infirmities, Steve Young's concussions, Dan Marino's age, and the lingering skepticism over the arena ball phenomenon in St. Louis, Kurt Warner.

The revival of Jeff George's career, at a pay cut of millions of dollars, ironically summarized where pro football had arrived at the end of the century. It was already the most successful and popular game in America. It was also the richest and now it had maneuvered itself into a place that made it unique. The place is called parity, which is zestfully cursed and derided by most of the pro game's critics. And because parity is a word used interchangeably with mediocrity, it is also routinely ridiculed by most of the fans.

But in deep December of 1999, the mathematical chance of getting into the playoffs made riffraff teams respectable. Their fans sneered at the mathematics that made this possible. But they hung on to each day's news. The team somehow still mattered–Carolina, the Giants, Dallas, the Bears, for God's sake. The Lions got in after being pasted four games in a row in

December. Traditionalists wailed at the disappearance of "dynasties" of dominating teams. In the National Football Conference in 1999 the dominating team during the season was the St. Louis Rams, who in their aimless state the year before had trouble finding their way to the team bus and lost 12 games. A year later they won the Super Bowl.

So let's go to class. (Jaws will be the man at the blackboard.) Why was all this happening? Why did almost everybody ignore Jeff George when teams were dying for an experienced quarterback?

First we'll have to identify the primary agents of change in pro football, These are escalating player salaries and the salary cap. Now add free agency, which makes the better players high-rolling independent contractors. Finally there is the NFL schedule, which produces a competitive cannibalism in which the strong teams are forced to chew on each other while the weaker ones get easier meat. The college draft theoretically is part of this mix. But it's been there for decades, including the times when a few teams, Green Bay, San Francisco, Dallas and Pittsburgh, controlled the league.

A lot of folks think parity is wrecking pro football. I don't. Yes, there are millions of football fans around America who howl for joy when the league produces a superteam that leaves nothing but broken bones, busted glass and scorched earth behind it and makes ESPN's next list of the 100 greatest since Moses. But most of those millions of fans don't live in towns with a National Football League team. The fans in those towns don't want their heroes' broken bones in their backyard. They want a team that can compete, even if it means 8-8 in December.

And where does Jeff George fit in?

First, about those 8-8 teams in the playoffs. We need first to recall Jan. 1, 2000, when the millennium turned and 6 billion people woke up surprised to find the world still spinning.

The National Football League, on the cusp of the year 2000 playoffs, woke up to the sight of a milepost just down the road. The sign was *not* a surprise. It said that some year, not far removed, a team with an 8-8 record during the season will win the Super Bowl.

You can dissent uproariously from this proposition. But you'll excuse me if you're not taken seriously. Consider: It could have happened in 2000, and not because a couple of the playoff imposters, Dallas and Detroit, bungled their way into the post-season tournament. Review. At the beginning of the season, the consensus in Las Vegas and from Jaws and his confederates looked at the Minnesota Vikings, the Denver Broncos, New York Jets, Jacksonville Jaguars, Green Bay Packers and San Francisco 49ers as the hot nominees. The Atlanta Falcons, a Super Bowler the previous year, got some respectful afterthoughts.

To see how this worked out, let's consider the stunning perishability of power in pro football.

In Denver, John Elway retired, Terrell Davis was lost early in the season and, not long afterward, Shannon Sharpe also was disabled for the year. The Super Bowl champion's quarterback, its best runner and its best receiver were gone.

Denver lost four in a row to open the season and saw its season trashed.

In New York, Vinnie Testaverde, the veteran quarterback who'd taken the Jets to the AFC finals the previous year, went down with an injury in the first game. It took the Jets two months to become a competitive football team and they were never in the race.

And yet–

Despite their horrendous early seasons, Denver and the Jets were fundamentally quality football teams led by two of the most prestigious coaches in the NFL, Mike Shanahan and Bill Parcells, respectively. By midseason, with some of their injured players back, with Brian Griese maturing as the Denver quarterback and with Ray Lucas installed as the Jets' quarterback, the Broncos and Jets were two of the better teams in football. They were better than half the playoff teams, in fact. If one or both reclaimed most of their strength just two weeks earlier, they probably would have made the playoffs. And if you got Shanahan and Parcells that far, the door was not shut to the Super Bowl.

It will happen sooner or later. And what is all this telling us? That a little less than 10 years ago, the National Football League owners and the players struck a deal that changed forever the way the most successful sports operation in America is run. Television receipts were approaching Pentagon numbers. The players wanted more money. The NFL said, yes, but we don't want your salaries to put us in the poorhouse. So the NFL agreed to give the players a total of 62 percent of the league's revenues. The players, in turn, agreed to a salary cap. The salary cap limits the amount of money the league's teams can spend on their players. The cap isn't impregnable. It can be dodged with the payment of signing bonuses and deferring some of the money into the future. But the salary cap does essentially what the owners wanted.

What they wanted was to keep the league competitive from top to bottom by preventing the cloning of a football George Steinbrenner, the New York Yankee baseball owner who was taking his enormous television revenues and gobbling up all the star players he needed to win the World Series. Baseball has no effective salary cap. It also doesn't have much in the way of brains or bravery in its leadership. So Steinbrenner or Atlanta's Ted Turner will win practically every time. In football, the Dallas Cowboys' camera-hogging Jerry Jones may try to do the same things by turning the sale of NFL merchandise into a cutthroat competition (with the advantage Dallas) rather than dividing the gold equally. How that kind of scheme will affect salary caps isn't clear, but it's going to be a war in the early 2000s.

And it may change the most successful operation of corporate socialism in American athletic history if the NFL gets dumb enough to let it happen, which it probably won't.

So until then, what does all of this millionaires' collectivism, parity, have to do with the life of the fan?

It fills it with stress, suspense and about equal measures of disgust and hope.

And why is that? To begin with, it doesn't take a whole lot to disgust the fan. Usually a two-game losing streak will do it. The hope comes in if your team has been sucking dust for a couple of years or more. The whole thrust of the NFL's quality control is to level the competition with the draft, the schedule and with the salary cap. By manipulating their payroll with signing bonuses and deferred payments, the 49ers became a dominant franchise in the NFL. But in the late 1900s they found themselves in the salary equivalent of Alcatraz. They were millions of dollars over the salary cap and they had to unload. In the middle of that, Steve Young got hurt.

They finished among the worst teams in football. Green Bay didn't sink that far, but it was close. Atlanta lost the great running back, Jamal Anderson, in the first weeks of the season and went into the tank. What this means is that an NFL powerhouse can disappear into the swamps in one year. The teams are so close in talent (or lack of it) that removing one key player (particularly the quarterback or star runner) can destroy it. And why?

Because the salary cap prevents the contending team from paying big money for backup players at the vulnerable positions. An exception in 1999 was Buffalo, which had made plutocrats out of Doug Flutie and Rob Johnson, the quarterbacks. Johnson wasn't needed to put Buffalo into the playoffs, although to the mass astonishment of football people, he replaced Flutie in the Bills' first playoff game. And the Bills, of course, lost. The money Buffalo paid to maintain two multimillion dollar quarterbacks made the team mediocre at other positions. And the final chip in the destabilization of the strong pro teams, of course, is free agency. After a certain time in grade, the players can test the market elsewhere. Their current employers can compete for their valuable hirelings by extending their contracts and pumping extra millions into those contracts to show the players how much they are loved. Sometimes the club gives in to the player's contract demands, because part of the bargaining gets the team mired in public relations. It doesn't want to flop the next season and face the fans' accusations that the management was trying to win on the cheap. But often the club will lose the player to an extravagant offer it can't match, which is how some ordinary football players become millionaires.

So the creampuff teams, the losers the previous year, can vault into the thin air of playoff contention by managing the salary cap, by drafting and signing free agents responsibly, by getting lucky, and by playing the wallflower schedule arranged by the NFL for all losers.

St. Louis did it in 1999.

The Vikings had no such space to overcome. What they did have in 1999 was a squirmy situation at quarterback. Their team for three or four years had been one of the elite in football. One of the reasons was that its management (then led by the CEO, Roger Headrick and the de facto general manager, Jeff Diamond) had squirreled away their best veteran players and kept them from the claws of free agency and covetous competitors by fattening and extending their contracts. Among those players were Cris Carter, John Randle, Todd Steussie, Robert Smith and Jake Reed. It meant that most of their stars reached their prime together. It also meant that all this stockpiling pushed the Vikings into the jaws of the salary cap and gave them practically no room to maneuver in the free agent market when Brad Johnson, just two years earlier their designated messiah at quarterback, signed with the Washington Redskins. His decision left the Vikings with no experienced backup for Randall Cunningham, whose spectacular 1998 season forced the Vikings to extend his contract into the millions and beyond 2000.

George had been released by Oakland. Nobody wanted to approach the multimillion dollar haul he was making there. Under the salary cap restrictions, no team had that kind of money to squander on a vagabond quarterback with few friends in the huddle no matter where he played. Green didn't care about George's social status. He did know about George's arm and his quick release and his years of experience in the NFL. He also had a half million dollars that hadn't been burned up under the salary cap.

Green contacted George and said in effect: You're a good quarterback but with us you'll back up Randall. We think we're going to win. You'll be part of that and you never know what's going to happen in football.

In other words, Jeff George might be playing more than seemed likely in light of Cunningham's great season in 1998. George had been making millions and losing. Green offered him $400,000, incentives to make $1 million and a chance to win a Super Bowl ring—for which most of today's gold-plated ballplayers would trade all of their investment brokers.

George said yes to Green. Once he started playing in midseason in that clover field of offensive talent that surrounded him, George the selfish sourhead became St. George the Transformed, a winner, a team man. A dozen NFL personnel directors nearly fainted. And George had his million in incentives.

The big money stakes that shape the NFL today mean that every move involving players in the critical positions is a throw of the dice. If the dice land right the coach can walk on water. If they don't, he's a dunce. His team gets to the championship or lands in the pigpen and the coach and/or the general manager join the unemployed. With the player payroll shooting past $50 and $60 million, the mantra that Al Davis invented, "just win, baby," became the creed for every operation in football.

And so if the corporate ethic in football is now that cutthroat, is football itself—with its lush profits of the last 15 years—walking a tightrope over an abyss? If the country's white-hot economy chills out and the TV revenues start sliding, and the players stay greedy and the owners stay arrogant, could pro football be heading for an economic decline?

If you're developing any anxiety shakes over that possibility, let Mike Lynn offer you a sedative.

"Look," he said. "Pro football is a monopoly. The only place it's going is up."

Mike Lynn can show you a membership card in the lodge of pro football authorities. Here was a guy who entered the National Football League as an office butler for Max Winter, then the Viking president. This was in the early 1970s and was brought on with the departure of the architect of the Vikings' championship teams, Jim Finks. Lynn was a promoter and salesman and impresario-in-waiting. He had no pro football managerial experience when he came into the league. There also was no limit to his ambitions, his brash ingenuity and a hip-shooting style in the player markets. Within a few years he was the Vikings' general manager. Within a few more years he engineered a corporate power fight with Winter, won that and became the operating CEO. A few years after that he fought off a takeover attempt by Carl Pohlad, the billionaire owner of the Twins, and Irwin Jacobs, one of the boldest takeover manipulators in American business. He did it by recruiting 10 millionaires as the new Viking board, friendly to Lynn, of course. In time he got bored, yielded to Roger Headrick as the CEO and bailed out of the Viking management with millions of dollars as his share of the ownership and additional annual millions from Metrodome suite revenues. In the meantime he managed to give the Dallas Cowboys the equivalent of Minnesota's 10,000 lakes in exchange for Herschel Walker, the superstar who shriveled into mediocrity in a couple of years. It was the NFL's trading disaster of the century. Lynn survived it. So did the Vikings.

There is not much that happened in the NFL in his years with the Vikings that escaped Mike Lynn, including the schemes, the conniving and the bottom lines.

"You bring up the chance of a downturn in revenues," he said. "I don't see that. Even if that happened, the players and the league have a deal. The players' cut of the pie is 62 percent of the pie. It's still 62 percent whether the profits go up or down.

"But the next big movement you're going to see in pro football is the globalization of it. I mean true NFL teams playing NFL schedules in other parts of the world, competition between American NFL teams and European and Asian NFL teams. This is no daydream. It's inevitable and it's already happening. The satellite technology has changed everything. Right now in the NFL's development league in Europe it has created hundreds of thousands of European fans who know the game. A lot of Americans assume most of those games in Barcelona and London and the other European cities are being supported by Americans living over there. Not at all. I'd say close to 99 percent of them are Europeans."

Lynn for years was one of the godfathers of the idea that pro football could make it in Europe and Asia. He worked on the NFL payroll for several years in that capacity and later did some consulting. So this is probably a given: You're not going to live to see the day when pro football unhorses soccer as the frothing passion of Munich and Madrid. You may, though, see Peyton Manning throwing flanker screens against the Hamburg Hasenpfeffers, which presents a scary scene. You would hate to unleash to Terry Bradshaw on the Hasenpfeffers and watch him try to pronounce them.

One thing we're all going to live to see is the roiling economics of today's pro football. There will be more attempted shakedowns of the public by freewheeling new owners who buy their way into the gold mine. But if they can afford to pay a billion dollars for an NFL franchise, they can afford to build a new stadium. They can, but they'd rather not. They would rather send the bill to the tax-paying stiffs. That strategy will not be new. It almost certainly will be more brazen.

"It was primitive and wild. You felt a brotherhood and a shared strength that was electrifying."

—Jeff Siemon, recreating the pregame locker-room scene before the Vikings' last Super Bowl game.

The Brutal Mirage of the Super Bowls Past

*I*n the melancholy hours after the 1998 Vikings lost the conference play-off game to Atlanta, denying them a place in the Super Bowl, Cris Carter lapsed into a near catatonic state.

His depression was acute, his physical and mental exhaustion that severe. He had to be helped up the ramp leading from the players' locker room to the parking lot hours after the game. This was an experienced football player whose personal life, his spiritual life and his professional life were in order. He understood where his highest priorities lay. He had experienced personal and team defeat dozens of times and was aware of his recuperative powers.

But on that day in the Metrodome his highest priority, to the exclusion of all others for those three hours, was to play with such fire and force that he would reach the Super Bowl, that he would drive his football team to the Super Bowl with his will and leadership and his skills.

His team fell short by seconds and by inches, one field goal missed by his team, another made by Atlanta in overtime. And the one goal that had eluded this superstar football player, in a career filled with trophies and gratification, vanished in the paralysis of silence that engulfed the crowd in the Metrodome.

For Carter, for a few inconsolable hours at least, it was like death. And it took him weeks to regain his mental vitality.

Is the Super Bowl that consuming to the professional football player today–getting there, winning it?

Not for everyone, probably. But it has that quality of grinding obsession for more football players today than it did years ago. In the 1970s, when the Vikings played in the Super Bowl four times in seven years, the game was a premium event, all right. But it wasn't the earth-moving, straight-out-of-Genesis happening that it is today, when its visibility is impossible to escape. It doesn't matter that much of the country's fixation with it is a triumph of choreography. Its producers have managed to invest the Super Bowl with elements that somehow connect Mardi Gras and Armageddon, in violation of all known laws of physics. But the fixation is real and the immensity of the Super Bowl's television audience is real. For today's player, the psychological effect of making it to center stage of the spectacle, actually winning the Super Bowl, is powerful and lasting.

The clinical psychologist is free to demand, "What's this? You're not suggesting that today's football player has mentally elevated the Super Bowl to the point where winning it makes him whole as an athlete and validates him as part of the elite of his game?"

No, I'm not suggesting that. I'm saying it.

We're not talking about validating an individual's personal worth. This is about professional status. You can pick the metaphor you want. Winning the Super Bowl lifts the player to the summit of the mountain. It puts him into some kind of rough-and-tumble Valhalla in which the Super Bowl ring is his seal of membership and can never be revoked.

If you need evidence, glance at the hands of the players and coaches when they gather for an old-boys reunion. The Super Bowl ring is almost always wrapped around whatever finger is big enough to support its weight, which is somewhere between a barrel lid and manhole cover.

Does that kind of reverence for the ornaments of success make the player narcissistic and braggy?

It doesn't necessarily do that. It does mean that the player has gone to the mountaintop of the game he played and has a right to be proud of getting there and being rewarded. They don't throw those rings around like jock straps in the dressing room.

Getting there and not making it, losing in the Super Bowl, probably won't leave a guy emotionally wounded for life. Most of the players who've been there and lost, or lost at the gate of the Super Bowl, don't have the despairing response of Cris Carter in January of 1999. Most of them will mask the hurt behind the usual philosophical shrugs and macho defenses.

But of all the hours I experienced writing Minnesota Vikings football, I found the days of the Super Bowl by all odds the most absorbing. Part of it was the carnival daffiness of the game itself and the hucksterism around it. Part of it was the sight of professional football players dealing with the round-the-clock showtime and their mounting yearnings and fears; and finally their hunger to win it.

Most sports columnists I worked with hated the orchestration of the week, and still do. They rebelled at the police lineup atmosphere of the mandatory news conferences. Picture it: players installed at round tables, available for the alleged rapier interrogation of the authors. Mostly it was burlesque. Scores of the authors filled their daily quotas of news from the Super Bowl battlefield with sardonic copy flogging the National Football League for producing these vaudevillian shams, as though some actual news was happening. They hated it, but they did write, and the Super Bowl was all over their newspapers. All of which deepened their furies at being converted into toads for the system.

My defense against being abused by the system was to remind myself that I was lodged in a bridal suite hotel room, living on a royal expense account and being amused by the Manny Fernandezes of the world.

The Vikings played the Miami Dolphins in the Super Bowl of January 1974 in Rice Stadium in Houston. The Vikings came with Francis Tarkenton, Alan Page, Carl Eller, Jim Marshall, Ron Yary, Ed White, Paul Krause, Mick Tingelhoff, Roy Winston, Wally Hilgenberg, Jeff Siemon and stars of that ilk. Miami had just as many and a recent history that included the only undefeated NFL season in modern times and a victory in Super Bowl the year before. The Dolphins brought Bob Griese, Larry Csonka, Paul Warfield, Jim Langer, Larry Little, Bob Kuechenberg, Nick Buoniconti and (too many) others.

On the day of the first news conference, the players filed in at intervals, not loving the oncoming scenario any more than the writers did. Jim Kensil or another of the NFL's PR staff would announce: "Ladies and gentlemen, Mercury Morris of the Dolphins has now entered the room and will be available at Table 8." The authors snickered predictably, but the herd instinct took over. They behaved as programmed and filed toward Table 8.

I always found the best table, though, was the one where Manny Fernandez of the Dolphins was sitting. Manny was a defensive lineman who projected a shrugging, weary contempt for being abused by the marketing hierarchy of the NFL. The reporters gathered around him warily, knowing his reputation. Still, this question was actually asked, by a reporter who clearly had advanced through Psych 54 in college: "Manny, do your find yourself slowly building a hatred for Mick Tingelhoff of the Vikings offensive line?"

Fernandez replied with a salvo of silence, which pretty much conveyed his judgment of juvenile journalists. Another questioner built his interview on the bedrock of all programmed Super Bowl interviews: "Is this the biggest game of your life, and how much emotionalism will there be in it for you?"

Fernandez exhaled a breath of prolonged incredulity. "What big game?" he said, with a gesture of a man trapped in a room with contentious but harmless imbeciles. "Every game I ever played was a big game. What do I have to do to show that I'm emotional? Run out on the field with two rockets strapped to my ass?"

When Fernandez ran onto the field the next day, no rocketry was visible on his bountiful rear end. He may have played emotionally. If he didn't, the final score, Miami 24-7 as it was, would have been too gruesome to carry back to the Minnesota glacier.

For the ballplayers forced to cope with that surrealistic daily grilling, trying to be honest about the pressures put them into a dilemma that ultimately made Gary Larsen's axiom immortal in the archives of Super Bowl weeks. Larsen was a huge blonde Scandinavian, an ex-Marine who emerged from the prairies of Concordia College in Moorhead, Minnesota, to play for the Vikings for nine years. He was the other defensive lineman on the front four in which Marshall, Page and Eller got all of the attention and did most of the damage. He was also the only white on the defensive line, a racial distribution that furnished all of them with gag material for the sports banquets. In practices late in the season, all of them would wear brown cotton work gloves to protect their hands against the frozen grass and dirt. One day Larsen came out with a brilliant set of red cotton work gloves. He needed something, he said, to get noticed. Page, Marshall and Eller applauded. The red gloves stayed for the rest of the season.

In Houston of the Super Bowl that year, the media tore themselves away from Tarkenton, Chuck Foreman, Page, Eller and Marshall long enough to discover the introspective Scandinavian. Larsen was said to psyche himself for games by talking to himself fiercely and visualizing the Marines storming a hill.

"All right," one of the writers said, "no matter how you try to put this game in perspective, isn't something really on trial for the ballplayers as individuals?"

Larsen thoughtfully considered the merits of this suggestion. He said, "I suppose it's the biggest football game of my life. But I hope you don't think I'm a wise guy when I add one thing: We've sweated a long time for this, and a whole bunch of people will be watching on TV. But there are 800 million Chinamen who don't give a good goddamn about what happens in Houston on Sunday afternoon."

The reporters didn't think Larsen was a wise guy. I did question his mathematics. I would have guessed there were more Chinamen who didn't give a damn about the Super Bowl.

It was one of those macho defenses, obviously. But Larsen didn't underestimate the impact of the Super Bowl on him personally. It was going to be part of some future summation of his career that he'd make somewhere down the road. Even in the years of the Viking Super Bowls, spanning 20 and 30 years ago, the tensions in the minutes immediately before the game were loaded with high voltage. In 1977 I collaborated with Jeff Siemon on a book, *Will the Vikings Ever Win the Super Bowl?* It was intended to chronicle the team's first Super Bowl championship, if that materialized. It didn't. But Jeff's diary, the focal point of the book, gave readers a vivid probe into the mindworks of a professional football player, from the drudgery of summer camp, through the season and into the Vikings' Super Bowl game of 1977 against the Oakland Raiders in the Rose Bowl.

Siemon was one of the Vikings' premium defensive players, a Stanford man with intellect and inquisitive urges. Each day in the locker room and on the field was a curiosity to him. The game itself gave him huge stimulation. The diverse personalities around him, the players and coaches, fascinated him. He'd become a committed Christian, a prayer leader but one not given to public demonstrations of his faith in the style of many of today's believing players. Nonetheless he was one of the first pro football players to be anointed "The Minister of Defense" by the press corps. The title is so contagious that it has now become a kind of traveling trophy around the league, applicable to almost any player who can make it through a recital of the Ten Commandments.

From Jeff Siemon's diary of Jan. 9, 1977, describing the moments before the game:

"The Super Bowl is a different, bigger, grander kind of game. There's no trying to kid yourself about that. Now matter how experienced you are, the realization of the size of it starts to take hold of you during your warm-ups and the locker-room vigil. It was even bigger for us than for Oakland; you couldn't deny that, either. This was Super Bowl IV for the Minnesota Vikings. It was the first for Oakland in ten years, and it was a new experience for most of their players. We speculated privately in the week leading up to the game about what the public would say if the Minnesota Vikings lost their fourth Super Bowl. So psychologically we had a huge stake in this–to avoid ridicule, if nothing else. I'm not a hotbreath of an emotional player, but I couldn't agree with Foreman more." [Chuck Foreman, trying to stoke the team into a Super Bowl frenzy that it had avoided in the previous games, invented a slogan: "Let's Go Crazy." He added high-decibel sound effects from his stereo, and some earthy street language.]

Siemon again: "We'd built something different and closer in the past few months. And right now you could see it in the faces of the players. The unity and fever were real. I've never been part of a locker-room scene like the one before this game. [Fred] McNeill had brought his tape recorder to the locker room during the season and other guys followed with theirs, and we had constant din on buses, planes and in hotel rooms. Fred had one album he played over and over, and he put it on before the Super Bowl. It was from the soundtrack of a movie called *Car Wash*. I don't know the name of the song or whether it has words. But it has a special beat to it, and you could feel the emotion rising. We were ready in full battle dress and the adrenaline was surging. It was primitive and wild. You felt a brotherhood and a shared strength that was electrifying. Players started clapping their hands and stomping their feet to the beat of the music. It was tribal and ritualistic, and it had us on fire. The eyes got bigger and the hands were sweaty. I never thought I'd be part of a psyching-up quite like that. It seemed to take control of you.

"And then we went out into the corridor and onto the field, and the whole pageant hit you in the face. Chanting, roaring, the banners waving. The only thing I've seen to compare with were the film scenes of those massive German political rallies of the 1930s. You looked at a teammate and you could see his nostrils twitching and sense his blood running. Somebody lifted his fist and yelled, 'Let's go. This is the *one*!'

"All these months and all these years.

"I know I felt that. I know Jim Marshall did. I didn't know how well the man was going to play, but I knew one thing: He never wanted to play more in his life. His life was ballplaying, and this could be the culmination of 20 years for him. He lifted his fist and nodded to everybody whose eyes he caught. He lifted his fist again and fixed his chin strap. He was dying for the kickoff."

It came, and the Vikings went. They lost their fourth straight Super Bowl 34-14. The Raiders were bigger and probably meaner. Art Shell and Gene Upshaw on their offensive line outweighed Marshal and Page by 40 pounds. The Raiders had a bald-headed lineman, Otis Sistrunk, who was widely suspected of being the authentic Man from Mars. They had another defensive lineman, John Matuszak, who seemed to have been lifted from the psyche wards of pro football. One of the cornerbacks, Skip Thomas, readily answered to the title of Doctor Death. The Raiders were a team of football derelicts temporarily given safe haven by the lone wolf CEO of the club, Al Davis. Davis employed players like Jack Tatum, a defensive back who frankly prowled for wide receivers to decapitate. The victims formed a club of which the Vikings' Sammy White nearly became a member in the second half of this Super Bowl. The Raiders gave you people like Charles Philyaw, who could either have originated in the Bible as Goliath or come on loan from *The Addams Family*. Rivals maintained that George Atkinson, another defensive back, played like the Godfather's oldest boy executing a contract. The coach, John Madden, often seemed less a coach then the frazzled manager of a mental asylum. But the Raiders played hard and well. They also had skilled football players like Snake Stabler and Fred Biletnikoff, Dave Casper, Shell and Upshaw and more. In concert, they ate the Vikings alive. After the game somebody asked the future state Supreme Court judge, Alan Page, why he was so terse in reviewing the game.

"How many ways can you spell "ass-kicking"? Page said.

Didn't Page think the Vikings might have tried something different?

"Yes," he said. "We could have stayed home."

At halftime, with the team trailing 16-0, Grant had tried to rally his players. Grant knew all about the embarrassment ahead for them if they didn't turn it around. But he didn't know any more than the electrician's wife from Sleepy Eye, Minnesota, in the 34th row of the Rose Bowl, why his football team looked so indisputably lousy and the Raiders looked like Caesar's army. "We can lose this game," he said at halftime, "or we can make this one of the greatest comebacks in pro football. There's time to do it."

There was, but Foreman couldn't hear that. He was crying, his emotions were pitched that high. Some of the old lions of the Vikings might not really have believed jivey Chuck Foreman in the role of the spiritual leader of a "Go Crazy" crusade. But Foreman believed. He had tried to shove them, pull them and tough-talk them into a mood of eye-rolling zealotry. He'd run like a man berserk in the first half, but it was still 16-0, and it wasn't going to get any better.

Is the Super Bowl all show biz and make-believe fury?

Oh, no.

From Jeff Siemon, Jan. 10, 1977:

"It was over and I wanted to answer all of the stupid questions as fast as I could and get out of that awful little locker room. The room was so small and there were so many reporters crammed into it that after I showered I had to stand and dry off 5 feet from my locker because some of the reporters were crammed into that, too. I felt miserable physically. My hands and elbows were swollen, and it had been so hot that I was drained. I got through the postmortems and rode with my brother to our hotel in Costa Mesa. You could reflect then. It was the whole thing all over again. The game seemed to have borrowed something from Dickens' *A Christmas Carol*. The Ghost of Super Bowls Past. I thought our other Super Bowl losses were jarring, but this was worse because we'd paraded our eagerness and our goals in front of the whole country, and then we just got taken apart, as though we really couldn't compete with these people. With all the winning we'd done in the last ten years, that was impossible to swallow. I don't really know why we played so badly."

Siemon's misery and lament were unanswerable. Later in his diary he told of talking with Grant, having the game, the loss, put in perspective and looking into the future about how his faith would eventually lead him to find something positive in the experience. That is a considerable faith. Like the others, Siemon survived the emotional crush and went on to live fruitfully. But I had a reflection of my own. I'd witnessed too many of these scenes not to recognize the eminence of this one football game in the players' lives. After the Oakland loss, I rode on one of the team buses with Jerry Burns, the raspy but totally lovable elf who coordinated the team's offense. "I've got a couple of beers in my room," he said. "We can split them." He started to open his can and then walked over to the window. I waited for him to speak, but he was lost in the devastation of it. He started to crush the can, but it was full and that wasn't going to be a winner, either. He slumped and turned. He was crying. "It's hard, Jerry," I said.

He collected himself and said, "Yeah, it's hard. I'll tell you why. A lot of those guys are the best there is. Some of them are getting old for this—Tarkenton, Marshall, Eller, Tingelhoff, Yary, Ed White, Page, Hilgenberg, Winston, all those guys. They've got to know this is probably their last shot at it They tried their damnedest, I'll say that. Late in the game when you could see it was over, they were still playing hard, and they knew it was over, and that's where I wanted to run down there and tell them that I never respected a bunch of guys more."

No, the Super Bowl isn't only glitz and round-the-clock make-believe. Sometimes it can tear the guts out of you, whether you're Jim Marshall or Cris Carter, a generation apart.

"This guy is the most amazing young football player I ever saw."

—*John Madden commenting on Randy Moss.*

Again—The Dogged Pursuit of Futility and the Super Bowl— Starring Randy Moss

Jan. 2, 2000

Just about the time the world was receding from the global light show of the changing millennium, a new jolt of exhilaration enveloped the Metrodome in Minneapolis.

It was lit by Randy Moss' first strides against a Detroit Lions' cornerback, Robert Bailey, in this last game of the NFL's regular season, a dress rehearsal for the playoffs. The sight of Moss streaking downfield one-on-one against the Lions' defensive back dissolved the obedient hush that settled over the crowd while Jeff George called his cadence under the center. The customers needed no X and O diagrams to see the obvious.

Moss was running loose against single coverage. The Lions' cornerback looked stricken. The crowd sensed his panic. And quickly the pandemonium machine of the Metrodome, boosted electronically by the Vikings' audio manipulators, was revved up to the red line.

Like Secretariat coming out of the gate at Churchill Downs, Moss was running free after 20 yards and the cornerback was losing ground. Moss veered right toward the goal posts and George lofted the ball, a graceful spiral nosing down, leading the receiver. Moss caught it in stride. Bailey got a hand on him from behind and Moss flicked it away. You were tempted to say he did it like a young monarch insolently brushing off the footman. Which is the way he did it, sure in his power, in control. With a few more loping steps he was in the end zone, 67 yards from the line of scrimmage, and the Vikings won the game by a touchdown.

A couple of days later that play assumed a deeper, more human dimension, involving a six year old kid whom the crowd was unaware of at the time. It might have put Randy Moss around the corner in his discovery of a personal sensibility that was otherwise invisible in his first two years. Before we look at that, it might be valuable to get a professional look at that signature play by Moss. In the broadcast booth, John Madden struggled–but not very hard–to suppress his wonderment at Randy Moss' uncanny virtuosity as a football player.

Madden is not your goggle-eyed football junkie. But you could almost hear an under-the-breath assessment of Randy Moss: "This guy is the most amazing young football player I ever saw."

Later he said it out loud.

Allow a minute's digression here on Madden, because you've heard him as much as I have. His longevity and the verbal quirks he brings to broadcasting, the mumbling shorthand of his analysis, have begun to irritate some of the viewers. They don't irritate me. Madden in the broadcast booth gives me an extra invitation to the game, whether it's one of no special significance or the Super Bowl.

It's rarely an insignificant game. The networks don't assign their most visible gurus to the meatball games. He's good not because he knows the game utterly as a Super Bowl-winning coach. They all know the game utterly. Bill Parcells is the best coach in football, or was. In the years when he broadcast the game he gave you most of the inside football you need, and he was good. But Parcells is tart and sarcastic and cryptic and careful not to betray the tough love he feels both for the game and some of the players in it. You're not going to get both his mind and his glands into the game when he's in the booth. The Joe Theismans and Paul McGuires are amusing and knowledgeable but relentlessly gabby and Phil Simms is second to Madden as a trustworthy interpreter.

But here's Madden doing Minnesota-Detroit. In his shambling style he gets you into the huddle and on the line of scrimmage more credibly and more intimately than anybody else. When Madden does the game you can hear the grunts from those people and feel their sweat. The fact that some of the grunts come from Madden in no way offends me, just as I like this guy ignoring the usual niceties and exclaiming in fury as the Lions let time bleed off the clock with two time-outs left in the half: "That was stupid clock management by the Lions." Madden is roaring. He is personally enraged by this breach of professionalism by the Lions. He pauses. "It just wasn't very good." He pauses again. "What am I talking about, 'not very good'? It was absolutely stupid."

I liked that from Madden because it reinforced my own mystification in the face of what the Lions were doing or not doing. At unpredictable moments Madden will wander back to his coaching years to flesh out the game. He knows what worries the linemen, what arouses them emotionally and why the Lions' defensive scheme is an invitation to suicide and what the little defensive backs are thinking when Leroy Hoard comes pounding into the secondary with his 235 pounds and his knees savagely high: "I tell you. You're not going to find a whole lot of people who want to get in front of this guy when he comes out of that line."

Is that the way it is out there? Fear, even in the insides of professional football players?

It is.

"Those little backs," the runaway tanks like Mike Alstott and Hoard would tell you, "they'll tackle you. But they'd rather not."

And yet Madden on this day does not think the Vikings eventually have the goods to get past the St. Louis Rams in the playoffs. That view is tempered by the sight of Randy Moss jogging through the Detroit end zone at the conclusion of his pillage of the Lions' secondary. Madden doesn't bother with professional restraint. "Randy Moss," he says, "is a super, super football player. Robert Bailey might want to know what happened to the help he was supposed to get from the safety. If he was supposed to, it didn't come. There is nobody in football who can cover Randy Moss one-on-one, including Deion Sanders."

Madden saw that, but there was something he didn't notice. When he got beyond the field, Moss handed the football to a boy he'd never seen before. The Minneapolis *Star Tribune* explained later in the week how and why that happened. The youngster, Chad Knapp, has cerebral palsy. He was one of those kids who spends hours idealizing his sports heroes, in this case the Minnesota Vikings. He'd wear the regalia at home, the paint and all the rest. For this game he received a sideline pass through the intercession of a woman who was a Viking intern and the daughter of the kid's principal at an elementary school in rural Minnesota. Now here was Randy Moss, materializing out of his daydreams, handing him the football he'd caught for a touchdown.

It was a wonderful moment, a kid's fantasy world made real in a scene he would cherish, and one that would link his life forever with the football player whose jersey number he had practically enshrined.

The player said later, "I don't mess with a lot of adults, a lot of grownups when it comes to autographs and things like that. But I saw the guy cheering for me. So why not go over and give him the game ball?"

There may have been a prologue to the story, from a year before in Tennessee.

Randy Moss' temperament and his attitudes are as much part of the daily scrutiny of media types as his extraordinary powers as an athlete. From the start of his two-year career, beginning with the bombshell Monday night when he dismantled the Green Bay Packers and became a national figure, the personal portrait of Randy Moss offered scant excuse for public adulation. It ran against the grain of the superb plays that only he seemed capable of making.

There were games, interludes when the Vikings' game scheme or the quarterback seemed—to Randy Moss—to be ignoring him. He responded by sulking. There were moments in a game when he played as though bored. Later he publicly acknowledged that he *was* bored. There was a play when Moss seemed to be jogging toward the Viking bench with a play still in progress but not involving Randy Moss. That was no illusion. That's what he was doing. There were plays in which he was running down the sidelines with the football and it was obvious he couldn't avoid an oncoming tackler. Randy Moss would then casually step out of bounds before a collision that might have given him an extra yard.

Why not, the kid superman could rationalize it privately. Others do it. Football martyrs end up in traction. The ones who get into the end zone have two healthy legs and ribs that are intact. Moss is aware that some football players do not play by this more convenient standard. Knowing that the old pros frown on it is not going to cloud his day or dictate his behavior on the field. Nor would it change his opinion of Randy Moss the football player: He knew there was practically nothing he couldn't do on the football field and that he delivered whenever he was asked or allowed to deliver.

That is a comfortable philosophy. Is it justified by the evidence on the field? John Madden, again. "If Randy Moss is involved, there is no play in the game that can't be turned into a touchdown."

That includes Randy Moss playing whatever position that seems within his range of football skills, which are almost beyond limit. Late in the season, possibly to ease Moss' spasms of boredom, the Vikings put in a reverse that wound up with the most explosive receiver in football (Moss) throwing a pass into the end zone to his mentor and sometimes exasperated godfather, Cris Carter. The play naturally went for a touchdown. Afterwards, Moss was asked he could also play quarterback in the NFL. He considered this proposition seriously. He thought it might take a couple of years but he could probably handle it. He also believes he could play pro basketball in the NBA.

Could he?

"He probably could, " said Jason Williams, the showboat point guard of the Sacramento Kings and a former teammate of Moss.

Public approval has clearly never struck this young man as a bedrock source of human happiness and self-esteem. He obviously has the public's acclaim and its awe. The public's love lags behind on his list of personal needs or gratifications. Yet his personal behavior with the Vikings off the field has been relatively impeccable, nothing to justify the knee-jerk anxieties of NFL scouts who black-flagged him in the draft because of his earlier delinquencies.

Cris Carter quietly escorted Moss into the realities of professional football and tried to deal with some of his indifference to public attitudes. "Randy has a lot of work to do about who he is and who he can be," Carter said. "But you have to remember that he grew up without any male authority in his house. Values that many people learn early came, and will come, later for him. He'll be OK, and he's already one great football player."

Values do come later. In December of 1999, the Vikings defeated Tennessee in a game that meant nothing for the playoffs. Moss and the others were walking off the field. A boy came to him and asked for an autograph.

Moss kept walking, refusing the autograph.

One of the Viking insiders, not in management or coaching, noticed. He approached the player unobtrusively and offered a thought.

"Randy," he said. "You're a major sports personality. Everybody who watches football on TV knows you. You might think a little about how people respond to you. That kid. I don't think it would have cost you much time to sign his program. If there was a mob down there, no way you should be signing autographs for all of them. But one or two kids–people would like to know that you took the time. Think about it."

Striding through the end zone against the Lions a year later, Randy Moss might have recalled that conversation. Maybe the wisdom and good will of it might have reached him and influenced him on the day the insider talked to him. Or it might have been something Cris Carter said. The young man has an absorbing mind. It might be wary today, impulsive tomorrow. Trust does not come quickly to a young man carrying the emotional sores of childhood. Carter has his trust, and Dennis Green. He may need more.

The Monday after the Lions game, my sauna partner was back in the hunt at the athletic club. He said:

"You saw that play where Randy Moss scored the touchdown. I don't care how young he is. He looked like a man playing against children on that play. How many players did you see in the early years before they were called great?"

With the Vikings probably Page and Tarkenton, Eller and Yary. With other teams, Joe Montana, Walter Payton, Gale Sayers, Lawrence Taylor, Eric Dickerson, Dan Marino, John Elway, Jerry Rice, Roger Staubach, Emmitt Smith, Deion Sanders, people like that.

"Did any of them leave the impression on you that Moss has?"

No. None of them could take over a game as suddenly and decisively as Moss, if the defenses allow him those four or five touches of the football, and sometimes if they don't. He can win a game simply by lining up. If they try to surround him, and you've got other winning receivers on the team, the others will get the touchdowns. The result is pretty much the same. If they're doubling him or tripling him at the height of his leap, the chances are fair that Moss will come down with the ball. If he doesn't the chances are 1 out of 3 that he'll get an interference call in his favor. It doesn't matter if he catches the ball for 50 yards or gets interfered with for 50 yards. It's still 50 yards.

"Do you think the officials are influenced by his reputation and might give him the benefit on some of their calls?"

They are and they do.

"So how do you describe this guy?"

The vocabulary is limited. You can call him uniquely talented, but a dozen players have talent at rare levels. You can call him phenomenal, but that makes him sound like he's from Krypton, which is just too far from West Virginia. You can call him a superstar, which he is for all of his youth and attitudes.

"Are you saying this guy is so good we need to invent new superlatives?"

God, don't go in that direction. To me, Moss is simply a prodigy, meaning this is a man who brings to athletics an extravagance of skills and instincts and gifts. He is so aware of them and confident in them that he can play with the effortless arrogance that seems to set him apart from the others. It drives defensive players up a wall. I've never seen a young player whose mere presence on the field creates such instant fear.

"Is he unbeatable then?"

Oh, no. He often plays carelessly and gets sloppy. Sometimes he's moping enough to play listlessly. He needs the right quarterback with a powerful arm, and he may not always have that. On a mediocre team, his self-centered view of his world could easily tear the team apart. I don't think, for example, that he's going to play for the Vikings very long. With all the money he's going to command, they may not have much left for the others. Texas, Florida or New York may ultimately be his place.

"Should we build a stadium to keep Randy Moss?"

No. Let Red McCombs build the stadium.

"Throwing out the superlatives, what do you really think of Randy Moss?"

He's a helluva football player. About the rest of Randy Moss—he can grow. If you ever get a Randy Moss in his prime, with the football disposition and the emotional maturity of an Emmitt Smith or Walter Payton, they wouldn't find enough money to pay him what he'd be worth to his team and to his game.

"I had nobody downfield. And then I saw Robert [Smith] out there, and he was all I had. . . just as I threw he turned his head, caught the ball and was gone."

–*Jeff George, ecstatic over quarterbacking a team loaded with Pro Bowl firepower.*

Again—The Dogged Pursuit of Futility and the Super Bowl—Starring Robert Smith

Jan. 9, 2000

Someplace between July and January there's a day of a love feast in the life of any football team with serious ambitions to stake out a piece of immortality, meaning the Super Bowl.

The Minnesota Vikings of 1969 experienced it the day they beat Cleveland in the polar wind-chill of Metropolitan Stadium to reach the Super Bowl for the first time. The races of football came together—white, African-American, Hispanic—to glory in this moment of their football brotherhood. And Joe Kapp emotionally refused his team's Most Valuable Player Award, declaring: "There's no Santa Claus, and there's no red-nosed reindeer and there's no most valuable player, either. We're in this together. It's 40 for 60." Forty players (the squad limit then) for 60 minutes.

It was a stirring mantra to carry into the Super Bowl of 1970 in New Orleans.

And the Vikings were mauled 23-7 by Kansas City.

Love and brotherhood saturated the locker room of the 1976 Vikings locker room to begin their pilgrimage to Pasadena, California, for the team's fourth Super Bowl. "Let it all hang out," Chuck Foreman howled. "Let's Go Crazy."

In the locker room they did. On the field they went belly-up against Oakland, 34-14.

And now in January of 2000 the next generation Viking football team lined up at the Metrodome against a team of even richer tradition, the Dallas Cowboys, in a kind of landmark game for both. Here were the Cowboys, draped in the streamers of Super Bowl championships, three of them in the 1990s, but bumbling along at the turn of the century, playing in a crisis of confidence despite the presence on their roster of great or once-great players like Troy Aikman, Emmitt Smith, Deion Sanders and Larry Allen. For Dallas, this was a game that could have reversed the slide from power and forestalled the wrath of the team's egomaniacal owner, Jerry Jones, who was about to fire the coach, Chan Gailey. Aligned against them was a team carrying the heritage of Super Bowl failure (the Vikings Past) and playoff futility (the Vikings Present) despite the presence on their roster of nearly a dozen Pro Bowl players like John Randle, Cris Carter, Randall McDaniel and Randy Moss. Joining them in 1999 were resurrected players like Jeff George and Chris Doleman. For the Vikings, it was a game that could launch them into their season of redemption and quiet all of the sniggering that had followed the organization's flops in the post-season.

And the Cowboys choked on their crisis of confidence. It never lifted. Robert Smith, Jeff George, Moss, the Viking defense and the brutal cacophony of the Metrodome crowd didn't help their digestion. Neither did Red McCombs' loudspeakers, which boomed the sound to levels that should have been banned by the Geneva conventions on inhumane warfare. Disarrayed, the Cowboys blew all of their first half timeouts in the first quarter. They fumbled into their own end zone and threw interceptions into the Vikings' end zone. It finished 27-10, a score which was an act of charity.

When it was over, the Viking veterans struck a tone of mellowness. They were getting closer. They were getting closer to a Super Bowl that seemed a joke to their nail-gulping fans two months ago. To Cris Carter himself it seemed so distant then that when the Vikings lost four of their first six games in 1999, he seriously asked himself, "Why am I still playing this game?"

But in the late afternoon of Sunday, Jan. 9, 2000, the Super Bowl was not so wild a vision. Oddly, Chris Doleman might have been a better fit to personify the idea of rejuvenation than the incumbent Viking veterans whose Super Bowl mission vanished in overtime the year before. He might even have been more suitable for the role than Jeff George, the reformed sourhead, or Cris Carter, the onetime dope addict who was now the team's inspiration and one of its superstars. Years before, Chris Doleman himself was one of those prodigies, a pass-rusher who was rangy, swift and belligerent, almost without equal in his early years with the Vikings. But he seemed to be playing the game in a vacuum, hungry for his sacks, competing with his fellow lineman, Keith Millard. Millard played like a caveman, beating opposing blockers to the spot with his speed and his recklessness. Doleman played like a terrorist, coming off the ball with a suddenness that reflected a gamble on every play, a split second early now, or late the next play, incurring offsides, mauling the quarterback. It was all part of his afternoon and his personality. It was Me. Chris. I play football this way, on my agendas. He was good, and sometimes he made the difference between winning and losing. But he was often disruptive to the team, and eventually wore out the management. Green sent him off in 1994. He played well with the 49ers in the pass-rush role. But he left the game after the 1998 season, evidently finished just short of the 150-sack level that would have put him among the elite of pro football's pass-rushers.

The Viking defensive line developed holes in early 1999. Green asked Doleman to come out of retirement. The financial incentives were modest. But like another of football's pariahs, Jeff George, Doleman looked at his fingers and found them devoid of a Super Bowl ring. He came back to no noisy acclaim in the Twin Cities media. He'd been a hard and angry man in the locker room in his earlier stewardship.

Among his achievements in his first incarnation with the Vikings was to receive the annual Turkey Award granted with dense sarcasm each year at Thanksgiving by the Minneapolis *Star Tribune* sports columnist, Patrick Reusse. Reusse's reactions to the Doleman of 1999 belong here. They offer a columnist's second look at a man he once lampooned. They also will open the way to a brief study of some of the yin and yang relationships that connect football writers and their readers, and connect the writers and the game and its personalities.

Patrick was a colleague of mine at the newspaper for several years. Today his columns and reports usually shake the last grains of sleep out of my morning stirrings. They will provide some quality writing and also offer suspense when I open the paper: Who is Patrick's victim today? Sometimes Reusse surprises me by being humane, a condition I usually prefer to public beheadings.

Reusse's columns over the year are a mix of acid, whimsy and arsenic with interludes of thoughtfulness and tenderness. When he's serious he is one of the more perceptive and persuasive sports journalists in the country. In the sports writing lodge Reusse's an agreeable guy, rollicking and snide, full of guffaws and the throwaway lines of a wise guy who knows his trade and the shams and self-indulgence of the athletes he covers. He also knows their genuine crafts and some of their struggles.

Most of us who've written opinion for newspapers have spilled into the trap of being cruel about it, casually or with unbuckled savagery. Some of us have done it less, some more. Today the rule seems to be more, and more by miles. The writer doesn't call it cruelty. It's bull's-eye journalism. Laying it on the line. Telling it the way it is. Or it's all in fun. For the writer it feels that way for the simple reason that it's more nourishing for his glands to write that way. It's also easier. One thing the "ripsmith" never wants to do when he unleashes his thunderbolts of judgment is to submit to the possibility that there might be another side to the story. The writer's litany of condemnation is less convincing if it's balanced by the view from the victim's side. You can call it stacking the evidence. Lawyers know all about it. So, the ripsmith will take the bungling player or coach and carve him a new behind in public. It's possible the poor miserable wretch wasn't a bungler. Maybe he was dumb. Maybe all he did was lose. It doesn't matter. Most of the readers will enjoy the spectacle. "What do you mean use a needle instead of an axe?" the ripsmith will ask. "Subtlety sucks. All those frothing fans on talk radio weren't calling to interrupt the commercials. They were calling because they were enraged at the stupidity and unconditional surrender they just saw for three hours on television." So the rule for the ripper is to throw some meat to the carnivores, the screaming fans. It's one reason why most opinion writers in today's sports pages will tell you in their private confessionals that it's better if the locals lose. If the locals win, especially if they win big, the public's attitude will shift from contempt to adulation in three hours. Not many people in the writing business get a wallop out of writing fan magazine fluff to feed the public's glorification of it's redeemed heroes. It's boring and professionally unrewarding. But don't send for a platoon of psychologists to treat the neurotic journalist. It's life. It's the way of the world. Consider your own predicaments. You don't want to spend the rest of your life congratulating the neighbor for his impeccable lawn and his generosity when they pass the collection plate at church. What you really want to do is call him a pious hypocrite who probably skims money at the local pull-tab operation. If you have those urges, you'd probably make a good sports columnist today.

Those attitudes aren't unanimous in today's sports writing. You can take your bites and still leave open the outside chance that the victim is a relatively decent human being who doesn't belch at weddings and really does know something about playing the game. In any case, what you're going to read on Monday after the game will probably be entertaining whether the opinionists are happily plucking at the local team's warts or congratulating the local heroes through tight lips.

Reusse is more entertaining than most and, because he is a bright guy with perspective, he has figured out a way to be more humane in his public hangings today and also found the path to occasional confession. He did a few days before the Dallas game. Patrick gave Doleman the Turkey Award in 1991 when he played for the Vikings the first time. He did it as a tribute to what Reusse saw as Doleman's "Me First" mentality and his anti-social behavior in general and his rules of contemptuous silence when reporters approached in the locker room. In fact, Doleman was one of Patrick's favorite dart boards before Dennis Green inherited that privilege when Doleman left.

Reusse knows football as well as most in the aeries of knowledge in the press box. What he saw in 1999 was a Chris Doleman who'd drained away most of his poisons and who at 38 was a football player and person of maturity. You'd hesitate to drag out the labels of dignity and pin them on a football player whose livelihood depends on crushing fragile quarterbacks. But it's about what I found in a visit to the Viking stalls before the playoffs and it's about what Doleman's old tormentor, Patrick, found in his more frequent visits.

What he found was that in his waning hours of football, Doleman had assumed the mantle of an old pro, thoughtful in looking at his game and the people and characters in it. By his deeds on the field and off he'd revealed, at age 38, something that wasn't there years ago, what it means to understand the idea of team. He'd worked his muscles and his mind into a place where he was as menacing on the line of scrimmage as he had been in his prime years. The difference was that now he had a goal far more magnetic and worthy than the self-serving ambitions that dominated his early years. He'd surpassed the 150-sack goal against Detroit. What remained was the Super Bowl. It would be his Super Bowl only if the team meant more than his ego. He seemed to play and to talk that way. And he could now be blunt without facing the accusation of being selfish. On TV, he'd said Johnny Randle was great playing inside the defensive ends, but he, Doleman, shouldn't play next to Randle because Randle tended to draw blockers in droves from the offensive line. And if Doleman had to battle through those, he wasn't going to be making any sacks. Randy Moss was a tremendous young football player, he said, but he didn't deserve at this stage to be compared with Jerry Rice or Cris Carter.

Reusse has never enjoyed the taste of crow and has rarely been seen eating it publicly. What he did in this column was to excuse Doleman's prior animosities and selfishness and to describe a different Doleman. It's doubtful that Doleman believed he needed to be excused. But in his old antagonist's eyes, tribute had to be paid to clear the record.

"When Doleman makes a play," Reusse wrote, "you see joy, but not the histrionics of this team's younger pass-rushers—certainly not the mad displays of John Randle. . . . [You saw] a comfort with himself and his status with the NFL that was never visible in those first nine seasons in Minnesota. The anxiety that would cause a player [Doleman] to campaign for the Pro Bowl and to get miffed at a teammate's honor is long gone, buried under an avalanche of accomplishment. . . . Chris Doleman has earned the right to be candid. He has earned a final, serious run at a championship. And after 15 years and 150 sacks, he has earned the respect that as a younger player he so often craved."

It was a good piece. It reflected growth and a willingness to understand on the part of the player and, it seemed fairly clear, on the part of the writer as well.

In the general love-in that followed the Viking victory over Dallas, Doleman was hardly the catalytic middleman. He didn't have that much time in grade with his new teammates and temperamentally he wasn't wired that way. Jeff George was the guy, although he didn't jump and scream earlier. When you throw three touchdown passes in a playoff game, you can be the man in charge of hugs and passing out gold stars. There was a state-of-the-art catch by Randy Moss, outmuscling and outjumping the Dallas safety, Kevin Mathis, after shedding the cornerback with the disdain of a bank burglar getting rid of a Inspector Clouseau. It went for 58 yards and 6 points. George congratulated Moss and offered an almost audible thanksgiving for landing with a team of pass-catching superstars. There were all-pros in front of him, he'd say. There were all-pros on the flanks. All-pros behind him. He was surrounded by them. All he does, he said, is throw the ball. But nobody was throwing it much better in 1999, or on January 9 of 2000, least of all Troy Aikman of Dallas. As it turned out, Moss probably pushed off Mathis. It didn't matter. The officials were now pretty much dazzled by Randy Moss and simply let him run and jump and push off. They seemed to be enjoying the show. So they threw the flag on Mathis. That didn't matter, either. When Moss goes deep, the Vikings will probably score, one way or another. The belief in that idea among the rival defensive backs and the officials is so fixed that the Cowboys played doomed, as though they were walking through the graveyard.

The hugs between George and Robert Smith, the running back, were authentic. Despite Moss, the Viking defense, George and the Cowboys' fatalism, the game was essentially belonged to Smith, the intellectual running back. He was the guy once defamed by the Vikings' fans as a practicing hypochondriac, always ailing with something, fragile and undependable. The ailments were real, the barbs were usually unwarranted. When healthy, Smith was and is one of the undersold super runners in pro football. He threads through microscopic holes in the defenses, changes speeds, cuts and slashes and then lopes into the open field with huge strides that obscure his sprinter's velocity. He drove the Cowboy defenses into flailing impotence. The statisticians had it figured at 140 yards for the game, plus a touchdown run of 26 yards from a pass in the flat that George threw in desperation and then in wonderment.

"Everybody else was covered," George said. "I had nobody downfield. And then I saw Robert out there, and he was all I had, and just as I threw he turned his head, caught the ball and was gone." He was gone because somewhere around the 10, Dallas' George Teague waited for Smith's fake. Smith faked with his shoulders and head. Just a twitch. Teague froze. The goal post would have had quicker reactions. And finally there was Cris Carter, jostling with the Cowboys' Charlie Williams a few yards further downfield. Smith was running the sideline. Carter watched to see which way Smith was going to cut, all the time muscling Charlie Williams with his forearms. Smith cut just inside the sidelines. Williams was lost. It didn't matter much which way Smith cut. Carter was going to bury Williams whether Smith went north, east, west or south or upside down.

When it was over, here was a team feeling in its marrow that it was headed for the Super Bowl. The prospect of playing the conference favorite, St. Louis, didn't seem intimidating. That was new. After all the undulations of the regular season, the quarterback change and the trials of its defense, this team seemed together.

Nothing much was new with Moss, though. A TV station from Germany, where NFL Europe football is popular, came to Minnesota to do the game. Somebody persuaded Moss to come on camera. "What's up, Germans?" the cool one said. "You all take it easy. The Vikings are going all the way."

Moss didn't major in public relations at Marshall. Noticing some of the frowns of the players who heard him, the cool one airily explained himself.

"Just a figure of speech," he said.

He might as well have saved the disclaimer. The quote was going to wind up on the St. Louis Rams' bulletin board for a mortal cinch.

Moss might have had a response to that if anybody pressed him.

Bulletin boards don't outjump Randy Moss.

"It's hard for football coaches to say out in public that they were at fault. It opens up things that can make the situation worse. But he'll tell us frankly if he did. A ballplayer appreciates that."

—Cris Carter on Dennis Green's modus operandi in admitting mistakes.

When Do You Hang the Coach?

Jan. 16, 2000

Three hours before the Vikings met the St. Louis Rams in the National Football Conference playoffs, one of my church pastors, Rev. Nancy Nord Bence, announced the program for the annual congregational meeting the next Sunday. In today's religion, one rule is this: Nowhere in the Bible is it written that the penitents can't be entertained on their way to heaven. So for the following Sunday the onward-marching pilgrims were offered an agenda that Martin Luther himself would have endorsed–church business, a chuck wagon lunch, a barn dance and a TV screen.

The television set was the clinching inducement. It meant reverential throngs were guaranteed for the annual meeting. The TV was going to put the Vikings in action in a fellowship hall for all parishioners who would have risked burning in hell rather than miss the game if the Vikings reached the conference title game on the brink of the Super Bowl.

The Vikings were not going to get there, of course. The church was spared a collision between mission statements and zone blitzes. What happened in St. Louis, the Rams' demolition of the Vikings, surprised a few million people in Minnesota. It probably surprised the pastor, the flock, Dennis Green, the peddlers of purple car pennants in 87 counties, and it surprised me. What didn't surprise me was the church's amiable but shrewd willingness to accommodate to the football frenzy. Nobody who looks out on empty spaces from a pulpit at the late morning service can escape one of the fixed truths of American society. Christianity, Judaism, Islam and all the others constitute one form of religion in this country. Without requiring pater nosters and potluck suppers, pro football is the other. If it's not quite religion, it definitely qualifies as a cult. There's one more difference. Organized religion makes demands on the minds and hearts of the believers.

Sunday pro football makes no demand on the mind.

Rationality ends after they toss the coin. Since the breakout of the fever in Minnesota 40 years ago, I've always sympathized with church people in their struggles to keep their parishioners' attention on divine intercessions when most of the parishioners were worried about end zone interceptions.

It reached a crisis in 1971 when the National Football League scheduled a conference playoff game between Minnesota and Dallas for a 12 noon kick-off on Sunday, Christmas Day at Metropolitan Stadium in Bloomington. Early in the week I got a phone call from Rev. Dick Smith of the St. Patrick's Episcopal Church in Bloomington. The reverend was both contemplative and ticked off. He said, "This is the crudest cut of all from the proprietors of professional sports in America. You'd think they'd have a little more sense or at least a little more understanding. This is a very significant day for millions of Americans, and noontime is a significant time for people who want to go to church on Christmas Day. Why does the pro football league have to put the church-going fan in a position of having to choose?"

There was at least an outside chance, I said, that television revenue might have some small role in the decision to play the game at noon on Christmas.

The conversation got down to the dilemmas facing football fans who had tickets for the game. They were sure to go the ball game but they were also going to be saddled with guilt about not attending Christmas Day services.

The reverend and I pounced on one solution simultaneously: a non-denominational church service someplace near the stadium.

"Father Smith," I said, "we will find a place to sing "Hallelujah" before the kickoff."

I telephoned Walter Bush, one of the owners of the Minnesota North Stars hockey team and the Ice Center arena a few hundred feet away from Metropolitan Stadium. I asked Walter if he could open the arena at 11 o'clock Sunday morning.

"What's happening?" Walter asked.

"The Vikings are playing Dallas at noon at the stadium. We need a place to pray."

"Why? I thought the Vikings were favored."

"They are. But we're not praying for the Vikings. The game falls on Christmas Day. We figure there'll be a lot of people there who'd like to go to church. The hockey arena is perfect. Can you open it? If you can, will there be any rental charge?"

Bush was silent.

Then, "I can't believe I'm doing this. Yes, I can open it. No, there's no charge. I've done a hundred things in that place. I've screamed and yelled and cursed at the officials, but I've never prayed there. I may come down to join the service."

"Bring a rosary," I said.

The next day I wrote a column announcing the ecumenical service. More than 2,000 people showed up at the hockey arena Sunday. Most of them were wearing the snowmobile suits and boots that were de rigueur for mid-winter football at the Met. *The New York Times* sent a feature writer who ignored the game and wrote about a worship service in a hockey rink. It was all about God in a building where a word of piety had scarcely ever been heard. Heywood Hale Broun was there from national television. Dick Smith printed several hundred service programs, not enough to go around. Lutherans shared with Catholics, Methodists and possibly a few Holy Rollers. Near the end of the 20-minute service, the reverend skittered out onto the ice in his robes to deliver his 3-minute sermon, the text from Paul's epistle about running the race, fighting the good fight.

At the conclusion we joined in three short hymns, led by a little choir from a St. Bonaventure church. The choir sang, as you must have guessed, in the penalty box.

To my knowledge it was the last time the NFL has scheduled a game at noon on Christmas Sunday.

Viewing the final minutes of the Vikings 49-37 debacle against St. Louis, and remembering the assorted Minnesota Viking playoff debacles of the previous years, I got immersed in the societal reaction to all these painful crashes of grown men playing what began as a children's game. Why did the game matter so much? And why, when it all went smash, was the despondency so deep (in the earlier years) and the abuse and scorn dumped on the fallen warriors (in today's football) so fierce and uncompromising?

There's one argument I've never quarreled with when promoters put the squeeze on the citizens for just one more stadium. The game, they will say, the team, can be a powerful force in the creation of a community; a community of hundreds of thousands, millions, bound by a shared passion. The passion is the team, its success, its march to glory. They won't say the community may not last. Obviously it is not going to outlast a 49-37 dusting in St. Louis.

Although a case can be made for asking the public to contribute a minor share for just one more stadium–the billionaire beneficiaries to put up the rest–most of the arguments for it are self-serving hash. The intention is to fleece the public with the promise of untold fortunes in economic benefits to the city and state and therefore the citizens. Bogus formulas are used to project those figures. None of the projections can ever be verified. The glittering promises of economic fortunes for the city almost never stand up under true tests of economic reality.

But the question was why do the fans react so violently or morosely when their love boat, the football team, sinks in the bubbles of a seven-touchdown barrage in St. Louis?

The community the team has built is real. Nobody who watched more than 50,000 people roaring rapturously and stomping their feet and waving white handkerchiefs in the Twins' playoff games in 1987 and 1991 at the Metrodome will offer any denial. After the American League playoff series in 1987, I talked to one of the Detroit relief pitchers who was on the mound in the midst of the din and wall-to-wall emotion. "Do you want the truth?" he said. "I was terrified. I felt like I was in a hurricane. The sound and all of that emotion, it actually hit me physically. The vibrations in that place. I thought I was going to get blown off the mound. No way could I pitch my game. All I wanted to do was to get the hell out of there."

That is community. It's hardly unique to football, baseball or the U.S.A. You want bedlam and ferocity? Actual insanity? Watch a soccer game in South America or in Liverpool, England. But the larger community that a championship-level team can build in Minnesota, for example, is healthier than that and goes beyond the stadium tumult. What it says is: "This is our team. This is us. We're together." The identification with the team, with its goal, spreads a true if fragile solidarity fusing the races, economic classes and the generations. For united purpose and hope and exhilaration it pretty much re-enacts one of the Crusades. That the source of this crusade and the solidarity is a ball team, not a war or a religious mission, doesn't make the feeling less real.

The one quality it doesn't have is mercy if the ball club gets wiped out.

But while it lasts, the shared exuberance and the suspense reach into all crannies of the electrified society. During the World Series one of the Minneapolis churches announced the text of the forthcoming Sunday sermon on the front lawn bulletin board: "In the Big Inning, God created. . . ."

And the same palpitations spread across the Minnesota snowscape on this day in 2000 when the Vikings played in St. Louis. With members of my family, I watched the game on TV at home. When you talk about a community galvanized by a football game today, you have to remember what the high-technology gods have done to intensify all of this. Throughout the game I kept getting faxes from my younger daughter in Iowa, wanting explanations. "Why didn't the referee review that catch by Carter?" the fax read. "He obviously caught the ball. They said he bobbled it, which he didn't."

I faxed a reply.

"Agree with you that Carter caught the ball. They didn't review it because bobbles aren't reviewable," which I admit now sounds like a title for a bad one-act play.

Fifteen minutes later I got the shortest fax in history. It said:

"Why?"

In the meantime the Rams were scoring touchdowns like Mongol hordes without conscience. I faxed back to my daughter lamely: "Will get back to you on non-reviewable bobbles. Right now I have to treat the casualties in my house."

The scene was essentially enacted in hundreds of thousands of homes in Minnesota. You could offer thanks if none of them were as Draconian as the episode in a Minneapolis suburban home after the Vikings lost their fourth Super Bowl game in 1977. The businessman-husband intended to watch the game with his wife. At a friend's request, he dropped in for a drink at a bar en route home. He forgot about domestic commitments and watched the rest of the game in the bar. As the score against the Vikings mounted, his disposition got increasingly ugly and inconsolable. The drinks he took at the bar didn't improve his condition. When the game ended he stalked out and drove the few blocks to his house. By the time he entered, these things happened:

The steaks prepared by his wife had shrunk to the consistency of White Castle gut bombs.

The flames had expired in the fireplace.

The husband's bitterness over the Vikings' defeat had left him enraged and speechless, equally indignant with the world, his wife and the Minnesota Vikings. He walked into their bedroom, packed a suitcase, wrote a note and left the house.

"It's over," he'd written. "I'm fed up. My lawyer will call you. We can talk about a settlement."

The next morning his wife got a call. "It's me," he said. "Can I come back?"

"You can," she said, "if you don't watch another football game for five years. That's the deal," she said. "If you break it we're done."

We don't know if the terms of the agreement were met. We do know that he never again had provocation to perform that nitwit act. To this day, the Vikings have not played in another Super Bowl.

There was a sequel to those Super Bowl losses, of course, on this day of Jan. 16, 2000, in St. Louis. Here were the Rams, happily rattling the chains of those old ghosts of the Vikings' past failures in the big post-season games. And thousands of Viking fans once more were picking at the warts of their team's playoff futility, asking the same question: Is there any end to it?

A friend of mine later raised a darker thought. "Is it us? Is there some kind of jinx? I mean it. What happens when the Vikings get into these games?"

My friend didn't really mean "jinx." The word she wanted to use was "curse." Was there some of kind of invisible sword of doom dangling over these people when they played in those post-season games? And if there was, where did it come from and who or what was the agent of doom?

I attempted a serious study of this proposition. I looked into the possibility that some of the old Viking gods of medieval times might have laid a curse on the football team. The original Vikings from the fjords and the longboats had a terrific winning streak, burning and plundering and all that. There is no record of the original Vikings in their horns and fur vests ever giving up 49 points in St. Louis in a raid on St. Louis.

Consider that. You could make a case that somebody like Thor got tired of those early Super Bowl fiascoes and decided the football team was an embarrassment to the Viking legend. Therefore, a curse. The football team would be doomed to play the rest of its games tantalizing its public and the betting line, getting endorsements from John Madden on Fox every weekend, but never winning the Super Bowl.

Which, when you think about it, is pretty much what they've been doing all along. The team's history does lead you to do some metaphysical groping: four Super Bowls, four losses. Three other times they could have reached the Super Bowl by winning. They didn't. In 1998, late in the game against Atlanta, they stood within a simple field goal of making it to the Super Bowl. Their kicker, Gary Anderson, hadn't missed a field goal all year. He hadn't missed an extra point. He was flawless, unbeatable. He was the perfect field goal kicker, as reliable as gravity. Against Atlanta, he missed, and the Vikings lost.

Was this a curse?

Probably not. If you really believed in curses, you'd have to hire a whole regiment of exorcists to treat the football team, and the Vikings don't have enough money under the salary cap to pay all of them.

No, the Vikings have lost enough playoff games using their own resources and imagination without needing some otherworldly intervention. The truth about the Minnesota Vikings playoff flops isn't as digestible to the fuming fan as all the theories to explain them. The truth is that reaching the playoffs means your team has been playing winning football. Excepting their formative years, the Vikings have done this when Bud Grant coached, when Jerry Burns coached and when Dennis Green coached. What this means is that through its 40 years of shifts in ownership, management, coaches and players, the organization has found a way to maintain some continuity and stability. That does not mean it has been shy on eccentrics. Mike Lynn as a CEO was a registered eccentric. So was Roger Headrick, who succeeded him. Grant was a cold fish, but his teams won. Burns was a noisy gnome of a guy, and his teams largely won. Green has the look and the furtive style of a man convinced he is under siege by scheming critics and slanderers. He can rarely bring himself to trust anybody outside his players, people he can control. So he isolates himself in his fortress, and his suspicions then become reality. He *is* under siege by the critics he has quarantined.

But his teams win.

This is not an apologia. This is basically the record of what this football team has done over the years. Its Super Bowl failures almost defy mathematical chance, but the team had Pro Bowl players at most positions then, and Grant was the coach. They still lost and they probably lost because the other teams had people who were better. In the times I have known them I've respected Grant, liked and respected Burns and respected Green without understanding him at all.

Their encounters with media critics and the fans took radically different paths.

The journalists absorbed Grant's Super Bowl defeats with the shrugging tolerance of a friendly jury. It was generally understood within the media clan that nobody was going to be more credible as a coach of the Minnesota Vikings than Harry Peter Grant. His teams won in every venue but the Super Bowl. They played a football that was disciplined and professional. Grant's personality was stolid, woodsy, predictable and threaded with old school principles. He therefore gave the journalists plenty of material to needle. But his results almost always put him in the playoffs. To the fans, Grant was a man from down home. His John Wayne demeanor, his history as a University of Minnesota star, his obsessions with hunting and fishing in the outdoors and his total absence of posturing, made him unfailingly popular with the Minnesota masses. About the Super Bowl defeats, nobody burned much energy blaming Grant. The crowd was never quite sure who or what to blame, but Grant was essentially immune.

Jerry Burns' teams didn't reach the Super Bowl but the media lodge responded to Burnsie's manic monologues and his breezy expletives with amused fondness. His team was streaked with neurotic characters both among its stars and its mediocrities. The critics condoned Burnsie and reserved their acid for the characters who made frequent appearances on the police blotters. These gave the journalists all the evidence they needed to satisfy their urges for prosecution. Burnsie was the last guy on earth to look for scapegoats when the team misfired. He was a sweet, brainy and infectious little guy whose scrambled profanities seldom reached the public. How in hell were you going to print them? Mike Lynn's colossal blunder on the Herschel Walker trade during Jerry Burns' tenure deflected any bile the fans wanted to unload. And Herschel himself, for all of his earlier achievements in football, was pretty much a cipher with the Vikings, not only in performance but in his personality. Mostly he was a big mystery from start to finish. He was often misunderstood, but he invited public sarcasm and he got it by the boxcar. Lynn and Herschel took the backlash. Burns didn't and wouldn't have deserved it.

So in 1992, here came Dennis Green from Stanford, where he was head coach, from the San Francisco 49ers, where he was an assistant, from Northwestern, where he was head coach, and from other venues. In practically all of them he was either a winner or he competed impressively against teams usually stronger than his own.

Among the Viking fans, though, he arrived as an alien presence and still is viewed that way. Fair? Probably not? But he reacted to the picture by burrowing deeper into his caverns of isolation and his defensiveness.

I doubt that it was of a matter of an African-American coach coming into an essentially homogenous stronghold of Nordic white folks and encountering cultural chill. The basketball coach at the university, Clem Haskins, was an eminently popular guy then. The Twin Cities were among the more racially progressive urban centers in America. But there was distance between Green and the public from the beginning. Green's instinctive wariness about surrendering privacy was part of that. What seemed to be his discomfort with mixing with the public was another. It didn't help when his team started losing in the playoffs.

The media annoyance with that pattern gradually escalated into ridicule, which prompted retaliation from Green in the form of silent warfare with the critics. The circulating poisons this produced eventually spread to Green's relations with the 10-member Viking board. They culminated with his vengeful, silly book threatening a lawsuit. The sale of the team to Red McCombs ended Green's war with the Viking management, but not with the journalists. Denny's teams kept winning during the season and folding in the playoffs. He made good personnel decisions until the Dimitrius Underwood screwup and the odd choice of quarterback Daunte Culpepper instead of the pass-rushing terror, Jevon Kearse, in the 1999 draft.

This and the deterioration of the Viking defense made Green an irresistible patsy for the savage critiques that followed the team's collapse in St. Louis.

He deserved the rap for the 1999 draft. But the erosion of his defense had more to do with the economic realities of pro football–free agency, salary caps–and with injury than it had to do with a misguided draft. Green was pounded early in the year for playing an inept Ramos McDonald as a starting cornerback. He was pounded later in the year for not keeping McDonald around in view of flounderings of the Viking secondary against St. Louis.

I thought the piling on of all those indictments was excessive and need-lessly abusive. But then, I wrote most of my football in a different era and I make no claim that the journalism of that time harbored a wider wisdom than what I read today. It might have been a little more merciful.

Most of the players themselves probably look at Green differently, because he presents a face to them that he doesn't offer to the public, or can't offer it temperamentally. Cris Carter became an adjutant to Green in the locker room in later years. You may be tempted to look on Carter's testimony as public relations smoke from an agent for the house. I wouldn't see it quite that way. Carter is a part of Green's private circle, but his talk is usually straight and therefore credible.

"He'll tell us if something happened during the game that he loused up," Carter said. "It's hard for football coaches to say out in public that they were at fault. It opens up things that can make the situation worse. But he'll tell us frankly if he did. A ballplayer appreciates that. His preparations for games are good. He's professional with us. Some of the players he's got are young with a lot to learn about life. He still treats them as men."

None of that is going put Dennis Green up for canonization in Minnesota. And if Daunte Culpepper doesn't work out eventually and the defense wallows, it's not going to save his job, either. And so, Green's decision to part with Jeff George before the 2000 season literally staked his future to the performance of the kid quarterback he drafted, Culpepper. He was saying "alright, people, you sneered at that call. So now here he is." Call Dennis Green's decision a nervy throw of the dice, or call it reckless and combative.

Football coaches can get rich today. They never can get comfortable.

"The hours after Walter Payton died created for professional football players, coaches and its followers a solidarity of grief and affection that seemed to wash away every conflict that divided them. It was an unforgettable moment. . ."

–Jim Klobuchar on the impact of Walter Payton's death on the game he played and its community.

The Price of Delirium

*I*n the summer of 1998, the wisecracking author of super-thriller novels, Tom Clancy, confided to the board of directors of the Minnesota Vikings that he had come as a messiah, with money.

He was going to rescue the 10 millionaires who owned the Vikings and lead them out of their corporate wanderings. While he was performing these heroics, he was going to make them even richer. In short, Tom Clancy would buy the Vikings for something in the neighborhood of $200 million, a very appealing neighborhood considering that each of the 10 Viking millionaires had put up less than $10 million apiece to buy into the franchise.

Clancy's generosity so impressed the Viking directors that they voted to sell to the swashbuckling author, practically on the spot. A deal was cut. In the weeks that followed, early impressions of Clancy were confirmed. He was decisive and brassy and he had plans. He had readers and connections. He had everything, it turned out, except money. Not only did he not have the $200 million, he didn't have a fraction of it that he could deliver as payment on the Viking franchise. Added to this, he was working on another book whose deadlines, presumably, were more urgent than his plans to overhaul the Vikings.

The Viking directors, all of them renowned for corporate sophistication and shrewdness, retired in a mess.

They revised their original invitation to bidders. The new one, when read between the lines, essentially said: "Football team for sale. Terms reasonable but present owners prefer more substantial instruments than Target credit cards and good book reviews in the *Sacramento Bee*."

What was happening with the Minnesota Vikings in the summer of 1998 should not be viewed in isolation from what was happening to pro football generally. Pro football at the close of the century had become a game for the corporate mikados of America. It was all about the money trail. That didn't necessarily make it bad for the people who watched pro football in America. It made pro football different and, in its dizzying economics and the rapid changes in the faces of the teams, all but unfathomable.

The changes at practically all levels of the game industry came suddenly and shockingly–ownership changes, management changes, coaching changes, player changes. The measuring stick by which a football franchise was judged successful changed radically. The team and franchise no longer were evaluated by how much profit they made, or whether the team was competitive. The teams had to win the big ones, the grails.

This had now become the only acceptable standard for success. The team not only had to win some of the big ones but all of the big ones. In the 1999-2000 season, the Minnesota Vikings advanced to the second round of the National Football Conference playoffs and then lost to St. Louis. The season was judged a failure by all gauges. A week later, the Minnesota Viking's offensive and defensive coordinators were gone, along with a cadre of other assistant coaches. It was a purge by the head coach, Dennis Green and possibly by the owner, Red McCombs. Green signed off on the mass evictions (which later included those of Jeff George, Randall McDaniel and Jeff Christy) in the full realization that another failure meant another purge, and this time the blade would descend on the considerable neck of Dennis Green. He may have been willing to admit to himself that if there was any single, all-weather architect of the failure, it was Dennis Green. It's not likely he'd make that admission, because head coaches don't usually reason that way. His plan was OK. He'd won before. He couldn't make the blocks or throw the ball or catch it. Others were paid to do that but didn't do it well enough or got hurt, and if enough of them were hurt, the team was toast.

So sometimes the coach under pressure would keep his job and fire his underlings, but head coaches in the National Football League don't fire themselves. After the 1999 season, Green Bay told Ray Rhodes to leave after one year and an 8-8 record. Chan Gailey in Dallas put his team in the playoffs both years he coached. He was fired. So was Pete Carroll, with a winning record, in New England. Jimmy Johnson couldn't bear the stress in Miami after four years and quit. Quality football players were dumped not because they couldn't play championship football but because their teams couldn't afford them. And they couldn't afford them because they had overpaid them two years ago on the gamble that here was the way to the gates of the Super Bowl–inflated player salaries. Let this overpaid cornerback go and bring in a new running back, and overpay *him*.

What was this all about, this Russian roulette finance, and bloodletting among the coaches? The answer was that football was so big and so expensive now that even the old limited-hangout, gradual landmarks of progress were no longer acceptable. The value of NFL franchises neared a billion dollars. Entrepreneurial cowboys enriched by the booming stock market and the merger frenzies began buying NFL football teams, first for the high visibility and the sheer electricity it gave them, and second for the money they could make when the excitement vanished for them and they decided to sell. In Washington, D.C., Danny Snyder put up nearly a billion for the Redskins and promptly started charging into the locker room to deliver lectures to the coaches and players if the team lost, disregarding the minimal barriers of good taste and logic. In Dallas, Jerry Jones clearly imagined himself as the de facto head coach–no prior pro experience necessary. In Minnesota, the extroverted car dealer and jock gadfly, Red McCombs, took over the Vikings. He boosted the decibel power of the Metrodome amplifiers to deafen and confound the Vikings' opponents and almost immediately began threatening the Minnesota public with the awful consequences of not building a new stadium for him.

Pro football had grown so big and so expensive that the 10 millionaire Viking owners who previously operated the team got tired of chasing the mirage of the Super Bowl. They even got tired of the status conferred by the ownership of a pro football team. Not all of it stroked their egos. They found themselves roasted royally for the Tom Clancy slapstick and found the CEO, Roger Headrick, a pain in the duff. They decided it was enough because they didn't know how or want to finance a new Kublai Khan-style pleasure dome for $400 million. They were convinced that a new stadium was mandatory to keep them competitive with the other NFL teams that were getting pleasure domes handed to them left and right by the legislatures and city councils. They knew it wouldn't be that easy in Minnesota. They also didn't feel especially good about ripping off their fellow citizens. And they didn't want to put up $20 million apiece to share the cost. To make it worse, they couldn't find anybody on the board willing to shoulder the 30 percent ownership the National Football League now required to calm the rolling chaos in which the Viking board was enmeshed daily. The NFL reasoned this way: One person controlling 30 percent of the action would provide stability and leadership. That might have been an optimistic assumption, and even if it weren't, they couldn't find a volunteer.

With Clancy back to his word processor and his terror conspiracies, the Viking board had a choice of selling the team to McCombs, the glad-handing Texan, or to Glenn Taylor, the Minnesotan who owned the Minnesota Timberwolves. Taylor actually could speak for more money than McCombs, and as a former legislator was politically well connected. Selling to Taylor would have insulated the Vikings against any threats by ownership to move the franchise, at least during the lifetime of Taylor's management and probably beyond. Taylor's prints were sunk deep in Minnesota. His increasingly popular basketball team was there. His friends, family and most of his business connections were there.

Taylor bid in excess of $180 million for the Vikings. He also accepted their approximately $45 million in transitory debt. Given the team's economic structure, the going prices and common sense, Taylor thought it was a good and prudent bid. It probably was.

McCombs bid $217 million plus assumption of the debts. To all but one or two of the Viking directors, there were no serious grounds for debate. As a former owner of National Basketball Association teams in Denver and San Antonio, McCombs had standing in the athletic community. He was a substantial business figure in Texas. His bid would give each of the Viking owners approximately $3 million more than Taylor's. People who are smart enough to be multimillionaires, or lucky enough in their inheritance, still fall in love with the sight of $3 million more.

I asked one of the outgoing directors, Wheelock Whitney, if the Viking board had thought seriously about putting the Minnesota public at risk of losing the franchise when the 10 Minnesota millionaires sold to the absentee owner from San Antonio.

Whitney is a straightforward guy. He said he did have some worries about that. So did one or two others. But the ultimate vote was unanimous for the car dealer from Texas.

I offered an opinion.

"I think they should have had more than a few reservations," I said. "I think the decision was deplorable. The Minnesota public is going to be hostage to the threats of moving the team for years to come. Its tradition and public support won't matter. Neither will the fact that the all of the previous ownership has been imbedded in Minnesota. The threats will continue unless the politicians here surrender and build a stadium."

Wheelock didn't necessarily deny that, saying:

"The directors truly believed that Red intends to keep the Vikings in Minnesota. I'll say this: For a long time I believed you could expect the public to underwrite most of the cost of new sports facilities because a tremendous bond can be built between the public and the teams. You've seen that and I know you agree with it."

I agreed with how powerful a bonding force it can be. I said I'd never been unconditionally opposed to some public role in the funding of a new stadium if it were critical to keeping a major league baseball or football team. I thought that need should be verified with a public disclosure of the team's financial condition, and the important part in the arrangement was the fairness of the formula. The bulk of the money ought to come from the chief financial beneficiaries, meaning the owners. Wheelock interrupted the monologue.

"Some time ago I changed my mind about how deep the public should be involved," he said. "Red McCombs says the standard formula now is that the club provides a fourth of the money and the public or other donors the rest. I don't agree.

"Red is talking about putting up $100 million out of $400 million. I think his share ought to be $200 million. But beyond this, I've been a Minnesotan from the beginning. I know the strengths of the community here. It's prosperous and it's progressive. It's major league in every way, from its arts and its technology, its medicine and education. But I have serious doubts that it can indefinitely support four major league sports here—baseball, football, basketball and hockey, of which hockey is the most recent. You might get enough fan interest. But a big piece of the new revenue is supposed to come from things like the luxury suites, and there's a limit to the number of corporations in the Twin Cities that can keep feeding those new revenue streams. There actually are fewer than there were a couple of years ago. Northwest Bank is now headquartered in California. Honeywell has made a major move out of the city."

If the Tom Clancy episode was a comedy and an embarrassment to the owners of the Vikings, there is more potential embarrassment in the sale of the football team to the Texan, Red McCombs. If McCombs does orchestrate a franchise shift out of Minnesota, the embarrassment of the former owners multiplies but would be trivial stuff alongside the betrayal of the

Minnesota public. Most of those directors prospered as Minnesotans. The football franchise was founded by Minnesota, meaning its citizens, and indirectly financed first by the outdoor stadium in Bloomington and then the Metrodome. The owners made millions on the sale of a team supported and partly subsidized by Minnesota.

Cavalierly, I thought, the 10 millionaires put it all in the lap of an absentee owner who now threatens to move if he can't make more money than he wants to by staying in Minnesota.

Maybe this is not an issue about which an ancient minstrel ought to be grieving. Maybe big-time sports have now become so powerful and freighted with money that those who look fondly on the game and its personalities should expect to be riding a carousel of madcap change. It is the kind of change inevitably fostered by the oligarchs who switch the franchises and overpay the athletes and in the process break up the teams, and then cash in when they sell the teams.

Yet it's the game, after all, that holds the public. I like the game, still. I find its action gripping, still not yet totally diluted by the hardball economics, the show biz burlesques and the gargantuan salaries. For all of the Cover 2s and four wideouts and the esoteric tactics of pro football, and the advanced technology with which TV presents it, it remains a compelling game played by highly skilled, powerful and driven athletes. It is a game that takes each play and can invest it with something from the chessboard, something from the battlefield, something from the theater and something from the playground of children.

The money players get today, even when it runs into the millions, is a poetic if expensive response to the unconscionably low wages that were siphoned out to the players who came before them. The players I knew best were those. I didn't hear much grumbling about the unfairness of it, nor about the feudal system that kept them bound to one employer for all of their professional lives if the employer chose to do that. That system ultimately was dissolved by the self-preservative instincts of the football owners. They understood that giving the players options to move was the only way they were going to get the players to agree to a limit on how much the clubs could put into payroll. So today, with football prospering as it never has, we have some sort of balance of wealth and egos and greed—not the tidiest basis for harmony, but that is roughly what we have.

It produces good and exciting football much of the time. It is a football now wildly unpredictable because of the movement of players and the disruptions from coaching changes and whims of ownership.

I liked the times of the '60s better. I liked riding around and listening to Ray Charles with a football coach eating himself alive because his inferior football team couldn't win more games. I liked a Paul Flatley coming over in the locker room and confiding, "I got to tell you what happened last night. . . and you won't print it, will you?"

I'd say, "No, not until you retire or confess." And it was a deal. I remember Ed Sharockman and Earsell Mackbee trading blows for five minutes in a blood-smeared fistfight in training camp, and leaving it with so much (if grudging) mutual respect that they never exchanged a hard word about each other for the rest of their careers. I remember Mel Triplett crying in rage and helplessness because the coach had cursed him racially, and he couldn't–in those years–do anything about it. I remember Bill Brown hitting the line at the end zone with such ferocity that he rammed the goal post stanchion in a half dozen games, coming out with concussions and memory loss and eventually prompting the NFL to move the posts back 10 yards to the end line. I remember Rip Hawkins and Fran Tarkenton alternating a round-the-clock vigil at a Bemidji hospital, praying in behalf of the team for the recovery of Tom Franckhauser, who was almost killed making a tackle in training camp.

Have the game's changes altered the game's appeal? Some of them have. Some are misguided or annoying and some are simply inevitable. The big money, for example; the squeeze on the public by stadium promoters, the exhibitionism on the field, the conveyor belt turnover in coaches and players. But you can mourn change until you get to be a grind about it. What matters more is that some values in the game are still strong, that you can still see personal integrity and class in the performers. This is, after all, the timeless appeal of the game. It is something you want to see beyond the players' skills and the high voltage of the game. And you do still see them. For a minute or so the camera focused on Tony Dungy, the Tampa Bay coach, after his team lost in the last few minutes to St. Louis in the playoff game. It was a television moment I'll engrave. The defeat denied Dungy's team the Super Bowl. When it was over, Dungy did not make the simple, obligatory handshake and walk away seething and crushed. He embraced the winning coach, Dick Vermeil, in what was unmistakably an honest gesture of congratulations. He didn't wave to Vermeil and vanish. He talked to him civilly, professionally and personally. He waited until the victorious

Rams walked past them, and he congratulated them individually. There was no bathos or contrived chivalry in all of that. It's the kind of person this man is.

He played and coached in Minnesota, collegiately and professionally. I've known a thousand Minnesota athletes or athletes who played here. I don't know when I've admired one more.

And finally you'd want to look at the life of Walter Payton to fully understand that the stereotypes of pro football sometimes are not adequate to characterize what the game can be. The National Football League asked me to do a retrospective on Walter for the Super Bowl program in Atlanta this year. I wrote a week or so after he died, and said at the beginning:

"Pro football is big and boisterous and sometimes brutal. It also is glamorous and rich and often heroic. And there are times when it is so big and visible it is simply engulfing. Pro football has earned all of those characterizations and more. One thing it rarely is called is beautiful.

"The game is about spectacle and the clash of powerful and driven men colliding with other powerful and driven men. But what happened in the hours following the death of Walter Payton transcended that portrait of the game. The hours after Walter died created for professional football players, coaches and its followers a solidarity of grief and affection that seemed to wash away every conflict that divided them. It was an unforgettable moment . . . He was a football player and human being whose death could reach a harsh and willful man like Mike Ditka and touch him with humility. It could reach undemonstrative football men like Bud Grant and touch them with tenderness.

"It could reach an uncompromising competitor like Mike Singletary and touch him with peace."

A football player, both in life and death, was capable of doing all that because of his decency, his honor and his greatness in what he gave to his game and to its public.

For all of its convulsions and its clashes of money and ego, it is still a game. And that is worth remembering. Sometimes the passion it receives from its audiences is comical in its intensity, and the attention it commands is a little foolish. But there are times when its drama is genuine and moving, and then it is worth the electricity it evokes.

About the Author

Jim Klobuchar's life as a newspaper columnist has been adventure. He's found it as a mountaineer on the great snow ridges of the Himalayas and Alps and in the lion country of East Africa. He was gassed by hippies in the streets of Miami during a political convention and survived a blizzard in the Beartooth Pass of the Rocky Mountains. Not surprisingly, he also found it in years of exploring the revolving melodrama of professional football, with its mesh of egos, artistry, and brute violence, its screwballs and its genuine heroes.

As a journalist, Jim Klobuchar has led two lives. He was for more than 30 years a popular columnist with the Minneapolis Star Tribune. He wrote daily commentary on politics and the shifting social scenes of our time, as well as human portraits that brought to his readers some of the loony pratfalls of life but also some of the rough nobility he's seen in it. Thousands of others knew him as a football writer whose reports and insights took them into the middle of the huddle and onto the scrimmage line. He wrote football then—and still does—with a range that gave sports followers an inside look at pro football in its nastiness and in the enduring camaraderie it has welded on the field and in the lockerroom. He's given them intimate profiles of such diverse football personalities as the tempestuous Norm Van Brocklin, Vince Lombardi with his simmering furies and will, the mischief and marvelous stamina of Jim Marshall, and the cold-steel craft of Bud Grant.

As an author, his work includes what he called the "unauthorized" biography of a football team, "True Hearts and Purple Heads," the story of the Vikings' generally hilarious early years when they were a refuge for some of football's incorrigibles and desperadoes. He also wrote "Tarkenton," a biography of the Hall of Fame quarterback and "Will the Vikings Ever Win the Super Bowl," based on the 1977 diary of Jeff Siemon, the Viking linebacker.

In 1984 he was named the nation's outstanding columnist among newspapers of more than 100,000 circulation by the American Society of

Newspaper Columnists, and was in the running for selection as NASA's journalist in space when the program was halted because of the shuttle disaster. Retired as a daily columnist, he continues as an author of books and as adventurer who organizes travel to the faraway places.